Decorating
for Christmas

Kasey Rogers and Mark Wood

Published by

krause publications
An F&W Publications Company

700 East State Street • Iola, WI 54990-0001
715-445-2214 • 888-457-2873
www.krause.com

Please call or write for our free catalog of publications. Our toll-free number
to place an order or obtain a free catalog is (800) 258-0929.

Library of Congress Catalog Number: 2003101340
ISBN: 0-87349-537-3

Photography by Kasey Rogers and David Skernick, and photo styling by
Mark Wood.

Acknowledgments

Whenever you take on a project like writing a book, you can never do it alone. And even though we have each other, we also enlisted the help of many others. For this reason, a special "thank you" goes to all of our California family and friends who allowed us to come in and make a momentary shambles of their living rooms, bedrooms, cabins, and schoolhouses. These include:

- Ed DeBevic's Restaurant in Beverly Hills, California
- Scott and Jennifer Rogers Doyle
- Sandra Hildebrandt and the StageCoach Inn and Newbury House Museum in Newberry Park, California
- Sue Ane Langdon and Jack Emrek
- Amanda Fox and Lisa Wilke
- Hollywood Forever Cemetery in Hollywood
- Motion Picture and Television Fund in Woodland Hills, California

Additionally, we extend a warm and grateful "thank you" to the many fine manufacturers and retail outlets, all of which are listed with contact information in the Resources section, beginning on page 126. Without their products and services, this book would not have been possible.

We are further grateful to our "good little soldiers" Bailey, Michael, Varsha, and Christopher, who helped us in so jubilantly being photographed.

Finally, we appreciate the efforts of everyone at Krause Publications, especially acquisitions editor Julie Stephani, editor Maria Turner, and graphic artists Jan Wojtech and Kim Schierl.

A special thanks to our friend and neighbor Lisa Curle for constantly getting those adorable kids together, holding props, steadying cameras and Christmas trees, and lending us storage space for thousands of boxes of ornaments, which were graciously donated by Krebs!

Table of Contents

Introduction

Christmas: What an exciting season—and it's such a time of memories! Each year as I begin to unpack my Christmas decorations and mementos, my mind wanders back to so many Christmases past: my first in California when I was about 3 years old and received a big-bouncy beach ball; my first roller skates at 8, the ones I fell and chipped my front teeth on; the cameo ring I received when I was 16 (and still have).

I remember the first tree after I was married. We decorated it with homemade decorations, and I still have a couple of large, raggedy, paper candy canes. Then came the children.

There's the little angel bib I embroidered for Mona's first Christmas, and there's the Snoopy picture I needle-pointed for Monika who was a Snoopy freak 'til well into her teens, and the key-ring I made to hold the key to Jay's first car. And, here's Mike's first mini-cycle MX racing shirt. It was white jersey and I appliquéd his name in black letters across the back and some black stars down the sleeves.

How sweet, the various Christmas ornaments the kids made with their names on them; the Christmas cards, pieces of sheet music, and children's drawings we thought beautiful enough to frame and hang through the years; the tablecloth and napkins, now slightly stained, that always grace our table; little corn-husk dolls, tiny angels, verdigris candlesticks, and wreaths.

It seems it was only yesterday my children crawled in their little Dr. Denton's toward these shiny gifts left by Santa. These are the same children, who now bring *their own* children (and yes, even *their* children's children) to share and tear open the presents.

Joyfully, this Christmas Eve ritual of bedlam always reminds me that the most important thing in life is to live and enjoy each moment to its very fullest and create beautiful memories as we go along—a trunk full of them. These warm memories are the fabric of our lives.

With all these precious old memories, new memories just keep asking to be made. It's a new era, a new time of life, new children added to our ever-expanding family.

So, I'll be making new treasures again this year and hoping the grandkids don't destroy them so they may have a chance to become tomorrow's memories.

And, on Christmas Eve, we'll gather 'round the old baby-grand as usual, and we'll raise a toast and sing a few Christmas carols.

Then, we'll crowd around our new-fangled computer to watch NORAD track Santa's progress as he and all the reindeer dash across the frosty sky, dropping off presents for good little boys and girls in almost every country in the world. (See page 23 for more information on NORAD.)

And, we'll all try to figure out exactly what time Santa is going to land on our rooftop.

Of course, before that happens, the Sandman will have sprinkled his magic and, having missed Santa, yet again, we'll all look forward to trying to catch a glimpse of him next year.

Sugar plum dreams to all and may all your Christmases become tomorrow's treasured memories.

Kasey

Kasey and Mark make friends with Santa's reindeer. It's nice to have friends in "high" places.

Candy Cane Christmas

*T*he beauty of a home decked in all red and white conjures images of the traditional candy cane and all the sweet memories of Christmases past. From a tree trimmed in red-and-white ornaments to a table adorned with vintage Santas, a festooned fireplace, and a candy-striped bedroom, you are sure to impress with your crafty decorating finesse.

The Tree

Choosing just the right tree for your family can be difficult. Whether it be a noble fir, Douglas fir, balsam, cedar or the old pine tree from Mrs. Milligan's side yard, the tree has to be perfect for your family and house!

One good rule to keep in mind; measure the space for your tree before you leave home. It always seems, no matter how perfect the tree looks on the lot, by the time you get it home it will have grown at least two feet taller and three feet fatter than the space you plan to put it in!

If you find you need to *trim* your tree, before you *trim* your tree, saw off any extra length from the bottom. So many people take a "little" off the top leaving them with no spire and what then looks like a Christmas bush.

And don't throw away those branches! Place them artistically behind mirrors or paintings or add them to floor and table vases! Adding to that wonderful aroma of Christmas.

Our living room is rather narrow but quite tall (ranging from 10 to 16 feet high), so we look for a "Pencil Tree" each year, very tall and rather thin. Besides putting it in the stand filled with water, we also secure it to the wooden cornice box above with invisible fishing line. You could secure your tree to the wall behind a curtain rod.

When decorating the tree, always start with the lights. We used extension cords with more than one outlet on them. These are easily found at hardware and other stores around holiday time. Ours had three separate outlets on each cord and we used four cords safely plugged into a surge protector. Start at the top of the tree and tie the extension cords loosely to the trunk.

The sap on your tree's trunk can harden, causing the tree to be unable to draw water. Saw an inch off the trunk before placing it in the stand with water. Check to see if it needs "a drink" each day.

Noël Note

Do not burn the tree limbs or needles in the fireplace. They may smell good but pine is filled with oil and highly volatile. They can be an explosive fire hazard.

Notice how Mark calmly looks at the price of the tree he really wants.

Noël Note

If you decide to add tinsel icicles after decorating, put them on the boughs one or two at a time, or else it will look like a mess. It is time consuming to sprinkle them so deliberately, but the results are always worth the effort.

Hot Glue Candles

We have been making these drippy electric candles at Halloween for many years. (See Halloween Crafts: Eerily, Elegant Décor, also from Krause Publications.)

This year, however, we decided to make smaller versions of our candles and dot them about the Christmas tree. After all, what better (and safer) way to get that Victorian look of a tree aglow with flickering candlelight than with "real" candles?

Materials

- 9 plastic electric Christmas candles
- 1 can red spray paint
- 1 tube Creative Beginnings Ultra Fine Blue Violet Diamond Dust Glitter
- 1 roll heavy-duty aluminum foil
- 24" length of 1" x 3" pine board
- 9 pennies (one per candle)
- Small handsaw
- 9 flicker flame bulbs (one per candle)
- Hot glue gun and glue sticks

1. Plug in that glue gun. You're going to be melting a lot of glue.

2. Test a bulb in each candlestick to make sure candle is working. Remove bulb and unplug candle.

3. Break apart base of plastic candle, remove, and discard. Unknot electric cord.

4. Use small handsaw to carefully cut the candle down to 3" or 4". (Be extremely careful not to cut through the cord.) Vary the heights of each candle for a more realistic look.

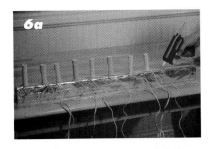

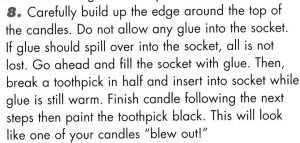

5. Cover the 1" x 3" board with foil and stand it on its 1" side.

6. Place electric cord along top edge of board and secure a candle in an upright position with a dab of hot glue, as shown (6a). Repeat, spacing candles about 2" apart (6b, 6c).

7. Beginning at the bottom of each candle, drip hot glue all the way around the candle and down the sides of the board in thin rivulets, as shown (7a, 7b). Work your way up the candle, allowing each level of glue to set before adding another layer above it.

8. Carefully build up the edge around the top of the candles. Do not allow any glue into the socket. If glue should spill over into the socket, all is not lost. Go ahead and fill the socket with glue. Then, break a toothpick in half and insert into socket while glue is still warm. Finish candle following the next steps then paint the toothpick black. This will look like one of your candles "blew out!"

9. When glue has cooled, place a penny over each socket, as shown (9).

10. Spray paint candles and allow them to dry (10).

11. Add a couple more *clear* rivulets of hot glue and sprinkle them with glitter while still warm. Allow to dry.

12. Remove decorated candles from board and peel away any foil that may be sticking to the bottoms.

13. Add flicker bulbs, place candles on tree limbs being sure to hide cords in branches, and watch the flicker bulbs make your tree dance!

Lights on a tree can be spectacular. Today, the fun seems to be in finding new and inventive ways to use lights. The Hot Glue Candles are a wonderful addition of light and act as ornaments as well. Mix them with other lights or make 50, 60, or 100 of the candles and use only those. And get creative like we did by using lighted tree topper stars nestled in the branches, as shown at left. (Better start in July, though— or get an army of elves to help!)

Snow on Branches

Here's a quick snow fix for trees. When finished, the overall look will be that of freshly fallen snow on the branches.

Materials

- 1 can DAPtex Insulating Foam
- 1 tube Creative Beginnings Ultra Fine Green Diamond Dust Glitter

1. Carefully squirt some DAPtex onto the tree branches, as shown at right, especially where two or more twigs come together. Allow the needles to poke up through.

2. While foam is still wet, sprinkle with glitter, as shown at right, and let dry.

Tree Trivia

Because the German Christmas tree has its "roots" dug deep in pagan religions, New England Puritans refused to accept it until 1875.

Still, trees have always been used in religious services. Early Druids, for example, worshiped the oak. And because fir trees were "evergreen," they became symbols of various gods.

Ornament Clusters

By purchasing packages of inexpensive plastic ornaments (the ones made to look like glass), you can create a different, fun, and economical way to make tree trimming a snap. These plastic ornaments are available throughout the Christmas season at discount dollar and 99-cent stores. All sorts of color combinations can be used from our red and silver design here to the pink, blue, green, and silver used in our Christmas DeLuxe Retro-matic section (page 44).

Materials

- Several packages plastic ornaments (red and silver in various shapes and sizes)
- Hot glue gun and glue sticks

1. Use hot glue to affix plastic ornaments to each other into large clusters, as shown in photo above left. Vary ornament sizes and shapes.

2. You may want to start with one "core" ornament, such as the long, thin one shown (2a), and glue smaller balls to it, as shown (2b). Keep in mind that each cluster may look different.

3. Let dry and hang as desired.

If you have selected a color theme in your holiday decorating like we have with red and white, why not extend it to your gift wrap as well? Choose only those papers and foils that coordinate and use several different patterns. Mix in a few vintage books and boxes of ornaments by companies like Noma and Shiny Brite for a nice homey-holiday touch. When buying these, be aware that vintage packaging can sometimes cost as much or more than the vintage ornament in the box. You just have to love those great 1950s graphics!

The Table

An absolute delight in red and white,
this tableware may be brand-new,
but it can still serve up memories
of a Christmas gone by.

Santa Transfer Tablecloth

Vintage tablecloths from the 1930s, '40s, and '50s can command high prices in today's collector market. Instead of paying premium prices, why not make a "faux" vintage cloth using clip art by Dover Publications? These dancing Santas from the 1950s photocopied onto a pre-made tablecloth bring the perfect vintage-look to your dining experience.

Materials

- Prepackaged 100% cotton tablecloth (to fit your table)
- Santa clip art (pages 118-123)
- 1 package Lazertran Paper (for fabric)
- Color laser copier, or home computer, scanner, and color printer
- Iron

Noël Note:

The percentage the images are enlarged depends greatly on the size of your tablecloth and your preference as to how big you would like the final images to look. It is probably best to experiment with a few black-and-white enlargements on a low-end copier to obtain the right size before paying for the more expensive color copies.

1. Wash and iron tablecloth.

2. Choosing any—or all—of the Santa images on pages 118-123, enlarge 250% using a color laser copier at your local copy store (such as Kinko's). Or, if you prefer, you may scan the images into your own computer and enlarge to the desired size.

3. Have the Santa designs copied onto the Lazertran paper, or if you are using your home computer, print the designs onto the transfer paper. Be sure they are done as a mirror image!

4. Trim to about ½" around each Santa.

5. Place images in desired spots and using an iron, press them into position. We found it easiest to place our Santa designs in the corners of our cloth, as shown at right, with one on either side, instead of trying to get them spaced evenly around the edge. With two Santa images leftover, we used them in the center of the long side.

6. We also found it fun to make several tiny Santa's and dot them about the tablecloth's center.

These little votive holders with candy swirls make perfect treat holders at the place setting. Ours hold candy "coal" made of licorice!

The red-checked dishes complement the tablecloth, as well as the vintage feel of the table.

Noël Note:

Why not take the little Santa images and put them on matching cloth napkins?

Claus Clues

Did you know Santa Claus never traveled alone? Besides eight (or nine) "miniature reindeer," dear ol' St. Nick used to visit the children with a character named Krampus. Known also as Pelznickel, Rumpleklas, Klaubauf, Zwarte Pitt, Hans Muff, and Black Peter, Krampus was a shaggy little devil with horns whose main job was to pass out the switches and coal to the bad children Santa visited. He was also known as Knecht Ruprecht, who wore tattered robes and carried a sack to put the bad children in! In Salzburg on December 5th, there are events called Krampus Runs where good children chase after "St. Nikolaus" and bad children get tossed in a sack carried by a masked man dressed as the devil. As for us, we'll just stick to sitting on Santa's lap at Macy's!

Decorating for Christmas

Chimney Centerpiece

What's more perfect for a tablecloth filled with Santas than a chimney centerpiece? The waving Santa next to it was an antique store find from the mid-1950s.

Materials

- 4 square glass containers (3" wide by 5" tall)
- 1 tube Aileene's Platinum Bond 7800 all-purpose adhesive
- 5 sheets of Scale Model Mesh Mounted Bricks by Houseworks*
- 2 packages Charcoal Grout by Clearly Mosaics
- 3" square x 2" thick scrap piece of wood
- 9" x 12" brown felt square
- Masking tape
- Sponge
- Scissors

These bricks are easily cut with scissors, but we don't recommend using your best ones.

*Note: It took five complete sheets of bricks to cover our glass containers, including bottom skirting and top lips. The size of the glass container you choose may require more or fewer bricks.

1. Cut wood scrap to exactly fit bottom of one glass container and glue in place.

2. Glue two containers *bottom to bottom* to make one tall, thin "chimney." The fourth glass container should be left as is.

3. Begin bricking the front side of the tallest glass chimney: Cut bricks (and mesh sheeting they are glued to) to fit outer side of the chimney. Make sure a bit of brick overlaps both edges. Glue in place. (If the brick sheeting is not quite tall enough to reach the tops of your chimneys, simply cut another piece and add to the top, lining the bricks up in proper order as you glue.)

4. Cut the sides of the chimney out of brick sheets so they abut the first set of bricks.

5. Glue side bricks in place.

6. Wrap bricks with masking tape as shown at right to hold them firm until dry.

7. Brick the medium-sized and smallest chimneys in the same manner as steps 3 through 6.

8. When glue is dry, remove tape and glue the uncovered glass sides of tallest and medium chimneys together, side by side. Then position the exposed side of the smallest chimney to medium chimney so that it is adjacent to tallest chimney. Do not glue the small chimney to the others because the weight will make it difficult for it all to stay together.

9. Add bricks to unfinished side of tall chimney where the medium one leaves off, tape to hold, and let dry.

10. Once all is dry, mix one package of grout according to instructions (if yours is too runny, keep adding grout until it is of a putty consistency).

11. Push grout into all brick areas, wait 10 minutes, and then wash away excess with a wet sponge. Repeat if any spots were missed, although a few "groutless" areas look very realistic! Allow to dry.

Noël Note:

It looks best if you trim the mesh around all brick edges so it does not show at all.

Claus Clues — *The term Christkindlein (meaning Christ child) became "Americanized" into the name Kris Kringle.*

12. To make bottom skirting, use two rows of bricks glued on top of the existing chimney bricks, as shown at right. Leave an opening so that small chimney can butt up against other two. Be sure to add bottom skirting to three sides of small chimney as well.

13. Cut four strips of bricks, each three rows wide and long enough to wrap around the top of each chimney to form the top lips.

14. Glue the top-lip brick strips on top of existing brick covering at top of each chimney. Let dry. Remember to only do three sides of small chimney.

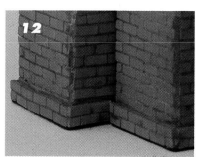

15. For the very top of each chimney, cut four strips, each three bricks wide and about 3" long and glue them on flat, carefully mitering the corners, as shown above.

16. Put a single row of bricks along the inside, top edge. If needed, hold all bricks in place with masking tape until dry. Allow all glue to dry before continuing.

17. Grout all bottom skirt and top-lip areas.

18. Cut felt to size and glue to bottoms of each chimney piece.

19. Add tea lights that will glow out the tops of the chimneys (or incense for smoke) for final effect.

The Fireplace

Extend your red-and-white theme to yet another room by really decking out that fireplace mantle area. Not only will you impress your guests with this fun look, but you're sure to win some points with the Jolly Old Elf. After all, how could Santa resist a fireplace festooned with so many vintage (and some not-so-vintage) renditions of himself?

Velvet Wreath with Ornament Clusters

Today, you can purchase plastic ball ornaments that look so much like their glass counterparts that it is virtually impossible to tell them apart—until you touch them. These plastic ornaments are quite inexpensive, usually a dollar a dozen depending on size, therefore you can use as many or as few as you want! Both this wreath and the Ornament Clusters for the tree (page 13) use these great plastic ornaments to create an elegant, affordable, and virtually non-breakable look!

Mark perched a vintage felt elf—the kind whose hands are permanently linked so he can hug his knees—in the wreath's center. These little elves, who look a lot like the Rice Krispies guys, can still be found at auction sites such as eBay or new at stores like Restoration Hardware.

Materials

- 12" polystyrene ring
- ¼-yard bright red velvet
- Silver spire plastic tree topper
- Red spire plastic tree topper
- 2 boxes large silver plastic ball ornaments
- 1 box large red plastic ball ornaments
- 1 box medium silver plastic ball ornaments
- 1 box medium red plastic ball ornaments
- 2 boxes small silver plastic ball ornaments
- 1 box small red plastic ball ornaments
- 1 silver "grape-like" plastic cluster
- 1 red "grape-like" plastic cluster
- Red thread
- Quilt pins
- Sewing machine
- Hot glue gun and glue sticks
- Small handsaw

1. Carefully saw through one side of polystyrene ring and set aside.

2. Fold velvet lengthwise, with right sides together, and stitch along edge leaving ½" seam allowance.

3. Turn sleeve right-side out and slip onto wreath.

4. Hot glue ends of wreath back together (secure with quilt pins, if necessary).

5. Turn under raw edges and whipstitch sleeve ends together.

6. Place gathers evenly around ring. Embed two quilt pins in the top and bottom of wreath to keep fabric from sliding.

7. Hot glue one tree topper to top of wreath. Use hot glue to build around it with various other balls and the two grape clusters. Repeat for bottom. Ratio: About 35 balls on top and 15 on the bottom.

It's all in the details. Decorating with candy is an inexpensive and wonderful way to ring in the holidays. These vintage ceramic treat buckets placed upon the mantle mimic the festive colors of Christmas. Begin collecting several new or vintage items in the same color scheme, adding to your collection each year.

More Claus Clues

There really was a St. Nicholas. He was a bishop in Myra in Asia who died on December 6 (St. Nicholas Day) in 343 AD. The bishop was a far cry from the Santa we know today whose legend got its start in 1822 with the famous Clement C. Moore poem, "A Visit From St. Nicholas."

In the 1930s, artist Haddon Sundblom of the Coca-Cola Company gave us our modern visual interpretation of the "jolly old elf."

Santa Heads Like Mom's

Ever since Mark can remember, his mom always hung one of these guys at the front door window.

After looking him over again, we figured he couldn't be too hard to re-create, so we made six of them!

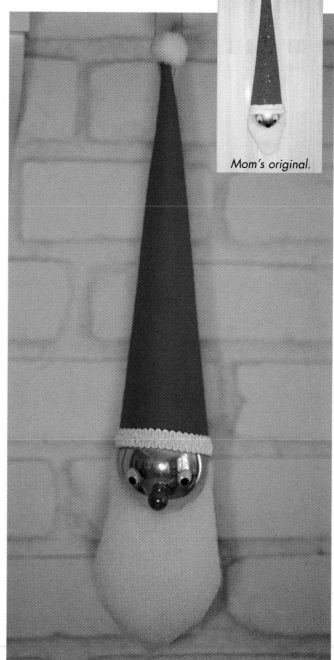

Mom's original.

Materials

- 6 pink 3" glass Christmas balls
- 6 red ½" glass Christmas balls
- 12mm oval wiggle eyes
- 6 red felt pieces (9" x 12")
- 1 sheet red poster board
- 6 white 1" pompoms
- 1½ yards white gimp trim
- ⅛-yard 1"-thick white batting
- Rubber cement
- Red thread
- Clear thread or fishing line
- Needle

1. Measure around top one-third of glass ball. Use that number as the bottom measurement of the triangle for Santa's hat.
2. Draw a triangle on the poster board 12" high by the number you came up with in step 1.
3. Cut out the poster board triangle.
4. Cover poster board triangle with rubber cement and place it face down onto felt.
5. Trim felt around the poster board triangle.
6. Roll poster board, felt side out, into a cone and whipstitch with red thread up back using tiny stitches.
7. Hot glue white pompom to top of hat.
8. Hot glue hat to pink glass ball so hanger is inside hat.
9. Cut white gimp to fit around base of hat (approximately 8") and hot glue in place.
10. Hot glue red glass ball nose and eyes in place.
11. Cut beard according to pattern, page 110, and hot glue under chin.

To hang Santa:
1. Double-thread needle with clear thread/fishing line, but do not knot.
2. Push needle through hat just under pompom and exit other side, leaving about 8" of thread on both sides.
3. Cut thread from needle and knot all thread ends together.

Signs of the Times

These rusty tin signs by the Mummert Sign Company (see Resources, page 127) are the epitome of a vintage red-and-white Candy Cane Christmas. Wired to the handle of an old shovel, they make the perfect outdoor decoration. First, put a tiny nail in the back of the handle for each sign so the wire won't slip. Then feed the wire through the holes on each sign. Thanks Marty—the signs are great!

Still More Claus Clues

Did you know you can track Santa's progress across the entire world on Christmas Eve? The North American Aerospace Defense Command (NORAD) has been doing it since 1957!

It all started when a Colorado Springs newspaper ran the Operations Hotline phone number for the Continental Air Defense Command (NORAD's predecessor) as a "Santa Hotline." Imagine the surprise on the military officers' faces when a bunch of children began calling asking about Santa's whereabouts.

The first call was answered by Col. Harry Shoup who quickly figured out what was happening and replied that he was tracking Santa's progress by radar. The media picked up the story and by the next year, a tradition was born. Phone calls came pouring in.

NORAD's Santa Tracking hit the Internet in 1997. It's live, it's incredible, and it even has video footage! Simply go to the Web site for details: www.norad.mil/NORADTracks SANTA.htm.

Or, you can call them at (719) 554-5816 for more information.

This has to be one of the most incredible ways to spend a modern Christmas Eve with children—of any age!

The Bed

Holiday decorating need not be limited to the living room and dining room. For those living in homes with no fireplace, the headboard (or footboard) of a child's bed can become the perfect place for stocking hanging. Even the Victorians were known to employ the footboard for just such a purpose. And when covered in a red-and-white quilt with a "Star Brite" mint for a toss pillow, those visions of sugarplums are bound to start dancing.

Santa Transfer Stockings

Materials (per stocking)

- ⅓-yard 36"-wide white felt
- 1 package red-and-white striped extra-wide double-fold bias tape
- Scissors or rotary cutter
- 1 package Lazertran Paper (for fabric)
- Color laser copier, or home computer, scanner, and color printer
- Iron
- Stocking pattern (pages 106-107)
- Santa clip art (pages 118-123)

1. Cut front and back of stocking from white felt using pattern as guide.

2. Choosing any of the Santa clip art images on pages 118-123 use a color laser copier at your local copy store (like Kinko's) to copy the images from the book. Or, if you prefer, you may scan the images into your own computer.

3. Have the Santa designs copied onto the Lazertran Paper, or if you are using your home computer, print the designs onto the transfer paper. Be sure they are done as a mirror image!

4. Trim to about ½" around each Santa.

5. Place Santa in desired spot on stocking front felt piece, and using an iron, press it into position.

6. Topstitch stocking ¼" from edge leaving top open. Note that the stocking is not meant to be turned.

7. Starting at top left side, sandwich the stocking edge inside bias tape, as shown at right. Stitch all the way around stocking.

8. Press bias tape smooth.

Made using the same Santa clip art used on the tablecloth, these stockings are reminiscent of the 1950s when felt was used for all sorts of holiday trimmings.

9. Starting again at top left, stitch more bias tape around top edge (side seams of stocking should lie flat toward the back). Cut bias tape ½" longer than needed. Tuck end inside itself and continue to catch with machine stitching.

10. For loop, cut 5"-long strip from leftover bias tape.

11. Fold one end under ½" and whipstitch to seam on outside of top left of stocking. Repeat with opposite end, whipstitching to inside of stocking.

Candy-Striped Pillows

This festive little pillow is really quick to make and brings a whole new meaning to finding a mint on your pillow.

Noël Note:

Bob's Candies out of Albany, Georgia, is a favorite supplier. If it weren't for this company, we wouldn't have any of the candies that so readily mean Christmas to millions. Bob's has been turning out the historic Christmas candies for more than 80 years. And even before that came candy canes, which were first made in the 1600s!

Materials

- ⅓-yard 4"-thick upholstery foam
- 1 yard red-and-white striped fabric
- 1 package clear cellophane
- 2 prepackaged 1½" buttons to cover
- Buttonhole thread in white
- Long needle used for soft sculpture
- Clear tape
- Black or red Sharpie marker
- Serrated edge knife

1. Use a Sharpie to draw a 10"-diameter circle on the foam. A dinner plate makes a great guide even if it is slightly larger than 10".

2. Use a long, serrated edge knife to saw the circle from the foam.

3. Cut a 20" x 31" strip from the red-and-white striped fabric. Stripes should be running in the 20" direction.

4. With fabric lying flat, right-side down, place foam standing on its edge in the middle of a 31" strip. Stripes will be at right-angles to standing foam.

5. Wrap fabric strip around foam and whipstitch ends together using tiny stitches. Fabric will now be extending from both sides of the foam circle.

6. Run a gathering stitch along top edge of fabric. Pull to close and knot off thread. Gathered center will fall in middle of pillow where button will go.

7. Repeat for bottom edge of fabric. Fabric should fit taut to foam insert. If not, cut gathering stitch on bottom and re-gather a little farther up the fabric edge.

8. Cover buttons with fabric, according to package instructions.

9. Stitch one button to top of pillow using the long needle and the buttonhole thread.

10. Push needle completely through foam to the other side (center) and attach other button. Knot off so buttons are taut.

11. Cover pillow in cellophane and tape ends with clear tape to resemble a giant Star Brite Mint.

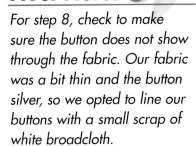

Noël Note:

For step 8, check to make sure the button does not show through the fabric. Our fabric was a bit thin and the button silver, so we opted to line our buttons with a small scrap of white broadcloth.

Don't limit the decorating to just the bed when there's a perfectly good bedside table sitting there feeling all forlorn and left out! Turn to the next page for instructions.

Vintage Wrapping Paper Lampshade

Shed some light on a festive scene with a decorated lampshade. Vintage wrapping paper is readily found on such online auction sites as eBay, but a favorite new wrapping paper is just as effective.

Materials

- 1 package vintage-look wrapping paper
- 1 Self-Adhesive Lampshade by Hollywood Lights (size of choice)
- 2 sizes matching gimp trim (yardage amount found on lampshade package)
- ¾" jingle bells (enough to go around the bottom of the shade)
- Red thread
- Needle
- Hot glue gun and glue sticks

1. Follow manufacturer instructions on lampshade for applying the wrapping paper to the shade. Be sure to center pattern on shade.

2. Once the paper is on, trim away any excess paper.

3. Cover raw edges at top and bottom of shade as well as back seam with gimp hot glued on top. We chose to add a smaller gimp in a contrasting color to ours for a bolder and more festive look.

4. With needle and thread, sew jingle bells approximately 1" apart around the bottom edge of lampshade to create the look of bobble fringe.

Vintage coloring books from the '40s and '50s always had wonderful graphics, especially on the covers. Try spray-painting an inexpensive frame red to showcase your favorite cover. The book need not be taken apart unless you want to frame some of the inside pages as well. The smaller picture is actually a tiny Christmas Seals stamp from 1954 that we found on a letter to Kasey from famed Hollywood producer Jesse Lasky. We had it enlarged at a Kinko's Copy Center and framed it in red, too!

Noël Note:

Unlike fabric, once the wrapping paper (especially vintage) touches the sticky shade, you are committed, so place it carefully. We started at the back seam and smoothed the paper carefully around the shade.

The tiny wreath perched on the frame corner was a snap to make out of some odds and ends we found lying around. Bits of moss, a few china flowers and leaves, a handful of red berries, and a small couple from an ornament broken years ago assembled into a darling decoration when hot glued to a small grapevine wreath.

Fake Cakes
faux Christmas

Photographed in the late-afternoon sun at the Stagecoach Inn Museum,
this potpourri of red-and-white candies, cakes, and yummy decorations
(without a calorie in sight) is sure to make a confection out of Christmas.
The possibilities are endless. When treated as real cakes, using paper lace
doilies and crystal cake stands, it's almost impossible to tell the real
from the decoration. Better put a warning label on these faux-cakes
though if you don't want a bite taken out of them.

Three-Tiered Peppermint Cake

This creation reminds us of a whimsical wedding cake done up in red, white, and pink. But since no one is really getting married, and this is really not an edible wedding cake, it does look great as a decorative accent in your kitchen and can even serve as a table centerpiece in your dining room.

- 1 each 2"-thick polystyrene disks in 6", 8" and 10" widths
- 4 bags Peppermint Swirl Candies by Bob's Candies
- 2-oz. bottle pink acrylic paint
- 1 small regular sponge
- 8 toothpicks
- 1 tube Creative Beginnings Ultra Fine Gold Diamond Dust Glitter
- 1 jar Darice White Glitter (looks like sugar)*
- 1 can DAPtex Insulating Foam Sealant
- Clear spray coating
- 12" cardboard cake circle with ruffled lace edges
- 12 bow-shaped plastic buttons
- 12 floating peppermint candles
- Hot glue gun and glue sticks

*Note: You will not use entire jar of glitter on this one project. There is enough in the jar to cover the projects in this chapter.

Noël Note:

You may wish to practice making small dollops on a separate sheet of paper.

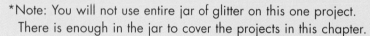

1. Sponge all edges of polystyrene disks with pink paint, as shown in top right photo.

2. Sprinkle paint with gold glitter while wet, as shown, and allow to dry.

3. Hot glue bottom layer to 12" cardboard cake circle and surround with small "dollops" of DAPtex Insulating Foam Sealant, as shown.

4. Add white "sugar" glitter while DAPtex is still wet.

5. Place three to four toothpicks in center of bottom layer.

6. Add a small amount of hot glue and center next layer onto first, as shown at right. Press down onto toothpicks.

7. Repeat steps 5 and 6 for top layer.

8. Add more DAPtex around cake edges, as shown at right, to keep any unpainted polystyrene from showing and add white "sugar" glitter while still wet.

9. Cover entire top with DAPtex, always adding white "sugar" glitter while still wet.

10. Decorate with more DAPtex, glitter, peppermint candies, and bow-shaped buttons. You will need to adhere the candies and buttons with hot glue.

11. Spray candies with clear sealant and sprinkle with glitter. A little DAPtex dolloped on top of them never hurts!

Berries Cake and Single Slice

This cake is a variation of the Three-Tiered Peppermint Cake. It has only two tiers and takes on an entirely different look with lots of faux berries to embellish it. It also varies in that there is a slice taken out to show the inside.

Again, a faux cake can bring the whole red-and-white Christmas theme into your kitchen or dining room.

- 2 polystyrene disks (10" x 2")
- 12 artificial red berry clusters
- 1 tube Creative Beginnings Ultra Fine Gold Diamond Dust Glitter
- 1 jar Darice White Glitter (looks like sugar)*
- Serrated knife
- 12" cardboard cake circle with ruffled lace edges
- 2-oz. bottle pink acrylic paint
- 1 small regular sponge
- 6 toothpicks
- 1 can DAPtex Insulating Foam Sealant
- Hot glue gun and glue sticks

*Note: You will not use entire jar of glitter on this one project. There is enough in the jar to cover the projects in this chapter.

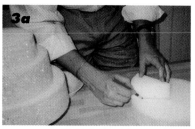

1. Sponge paint around edges of both 10" polystyrene disks.

2. Sprinkle Diamond Dust glitter onto painted disks while paint is still wet.

3. Remove a wedge-shaped slice of cake from one of the 10" polystyrene disks using a serrated edge knife. Use the wedge as a pattern, as shown (3a), and cut another slice from the second 10" disk (3b).

4. Paint edges of slice as well as cake edges where slice was removed, as shown (4a, 4b).

5. While paint is still wet, sprinkle slice and inside slice portion of whole cake with Diamond Dust Glitter. Let dry.

6. Apply DAPtex to top edge of one polystyrene disk.

7. Add three toothpicks and a squirt of hot glue to middle.

8. Center the other polystyrene disk on top of toothpicks and press down while glue and DAPtex are still wet.

9. Repeat steps 6 through 8 for slice as well.

10. Cover entire top of cake and slice with DAPtex and white "sugar" glitter, allowing DAPtex to "dollop" over top edges. Let dry.

11. With hot glue, place shiny red berry clusters as shown at left.

This small cake was created using two 4" x 2" polystyrene disks. Decorated in much the same way as stated above we used a small ceramic clown as the topper to this light-as-a-feather confectionery concoction.

Cupcakes

Much smaller versions of the full-size cakes, these faux cupcakes look just as sweet as an accent in your kitchen or even as a creative centerpiece on your holiday table.

Materials

- 1 can DAPtex Insulating Foam Sealant
- 1 jar Darice White Glitter (looks like sugar)*
- 12 cupcake papers
- 12 gumdrops, candies, or candy-like buttons
- 12 small snowflake buttons
- 1 tube red glitter
- 1 squeeze bottle Scribbles red paint
- Hot glue gun and glue sticks
- Muffin tin (optional)

*Note: You will not use entire jar of glitter on this one project. There is enough in the jar to cover all the projects in this chapter.

1. Fill white cupcake papers three-quarters full with DAPtex Insulating Foam Sealant. You may place the cupcake papers into a muffin tin before filling if you are concerned about the "cakes" maintaining their shape. The DAPtex will wash off, should any spill over onto the tin.

2. While DAPtex is still wet, sprinkle with white "sugar" glitter as well as some red glitter, and allow to dry. DAPtex will rise while drying.

3. Decorate with gumdrops, candies, or candy-looking buttons. Hold in place with a small dab of hot glue.

4. Use squeeze bottle of red paint to add dots randomly to top of cupcakes to create the look of "berries" or "red hot" candies.

Ice Cream Cones

Imagine ice cream cones that do not melt when left out! These non-dairy delights again make creative holiday accents most fittingly in your kitchen.

Materials (makes 12)

- 1 can DAPtex Insulating Foam Sealant
- 1 jar Darice White Glitter (looks like sugar)*
- 12 flat-bottom ice cream cones
- 1 bag red gumdrops
- 1 bag white gumdrops
- Assorted candies or candy-like buttons (optional)

*Note: You will not use entire jar of glitter on this one project. There is enough in the jar to cover the projects in this chapter.

1. Overfill flat-bottomed cones with DAPtex Insulating Foam Sealant and sprinkle with white "sugar" glitter while wet.

2. Decorate with red and white gumdrops, candies, or buttons, as shown at right. Hold in place with a small dab of hot glue.

Candlelight in the Snow

Mix and match the items below as you wish to create these candle-lit centerpieces. We found that DAPtex Insulating Foam Sealant is incredibly versatile and, with a little scrubbing, will readily wash off glazed china, ceramics, and glass. We do not, however, recommend using your best family china.

Materials

- Glass hurricane globe
- Crystal cake stand (to fit bottom of hurricane globe with room leftover)
- 1 box Krebs red glass Christmas balls
- 1 can DAPtex Insulating Foam Sealant
- 1 tube Creative Beginnings Ultra Fine Green Diamond Dust Glitter
- Candle
- 8 small flowers (fresh or silk)

1. Place a hurricane globe in the center of the plate.

2. Squirt DAPtex around the hurricane globe base.

3. Sprinkle with copious amounts of glitter.

4. Remove the metal crown and loop from the glass balls and embed them into the DAPtex before it dries. Be sure opening sticks up.

5. Fill the embedded balls with water and insert fresh flowers as shown into these unique little vases (no water needed for silk). We found that the shine was dulled on the glass balls after being removed from the DAPtex, so do not use family heirlooms!

6. Add candle and light.

Project variation with oil candles.

An In-Spired City

This centerpiece, great for table or mantle, reminds one of a Russian city. It is a decorating idea that utilizes most of what you already have in your home at Christmas and suggests a way to pull it together creatively.

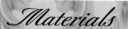

Materials

- 8 crystal and/or white candlesticks
- 8 red-and-white assorted ornaments
- Christmas tree spire
- 2 glass candy jars
- 3 bags Peppermint Swirl Candies by Bob's Candies
- Earthquake putty (museum wax)
- 30 plastic ball ornaments in varying sizes
- 1 "grape" cluster of plastic ball ornaments
- Hot glue gun and glue sticks

Noël Note:

Other decorative vases or bowls can also be used in your display—even small eggcups look great with an ornament placed in them.

1. Cluster several white and crystal candlesticks of different heights together.

2. Using red-and-white (or colors of choice) ornaments in place of candles, insert hanger ends into the candlesticks and hold in place with a little earthquake putty.

3. Add a few glass candy jars filled with brightly colored candies.

4. Top off the center with a Christmas tree spire so it stands above the rest.

5. For the clustered candle ring around the main spire, hot glue plastic ornament balls together to form a ring, building it closely around the spire as you go. The ring should rest on the candlestick when complete.

6. Add more balls of various sizes and the grape cluster to ring.

Eggcup Snowmen

Materials

- 4 white china saki wine cups*
- 4 wood or ceramic prepackaged miniature carrots**
- 1 package 10mm oval wiggle eyes
- 4 doll-size plastic top hats
- 1 yard red-and-white checked ribbon
- Hot glue gun and glue sticks
- Scissors

* Saki cups are sold individually at stores such as Pier 1 or Cost Plus.

** If you cannot find pre-made miniature carrots, make your own using a modeling compound such as Sculpey. Knead into carrot shape and bake as directed.

Enjoy an early Christmas breakfast with these guys. Afterwards, run like mad to the tree and tear into those wrapped goodies that are calling your name!

Soft-Boiled Egg Recipe

What's a decorative egg cup without the egg? Here is a quick recipe for soft-boiled eggs that will keep your guests hungry for more!

Bring water to boil in pot and slowly immerse the number of eggs you desire.

Allow the eggs to boil for three minutes, remove from water with slotted spoon, and place them into the eggcups. Serve while hot.

Noël Note:

To eat this rather warm snowman, remove hat and lop off the top of his head with a table knife! Salt and pepper to taste.

1. Hot glue a carrot nose to edge of saki cup slightly above rim.
2. Hot glue an oval eye to either side of carrot nose so each eye extends two-thirds above cup rim.
3. Cut ribbon into 9" lengths and fringe each end.
4. Knot ribbon around "neck" base of saki cup.
5. Place soft-boiled egg small side down into decorated cup, as shown below (egg recipe at left).
6. Perch top hat on top of the egg, as shown.

What's In a Name? Santa Claus ought to know. He has many names, among them: in Austria, he is Chriskind; in Brazil, it is Papai Noël; in China, Dun Che Lao Ren; in Denmark, Julemanden; in Holland, he is called Sinterklaas (an early version of the now Americanized Santa Claus); in Sweden, the kindly gift-giver is called Jultomten; in Norway, Julenissen; in Japan, Santa Kurousu; and Pere Noël in France. In Italy, the gifts are delivered by, of all things, a witch known as La Befana! Let's hear it for the Christmas witches.

DeLuxe Retro-matic

*T*his chapter takes an amusing look back at a time when almost everything was described as "DeLuxe" or had an "o-matic" tagged onto the end of its name.

We took wonderful retro colors, added a few pink poodles, an old Christmas card of Kasey's (with cartoons of "Bewitched's" Larry and Darrin), an incredible new product called Lazertran, a few candy canes and ice cream and viola!—instant Christmas DeLuxe o-matic.

Retro-Tree

Immensely popular in the 1950s, today vintage silver tinsel trees can command high prices in the collectors' market, especially if they come complete in their original box. And because you wouldn't dare put electric lights on a metal tree (you might as well be standing in a bucket of water while you did it), these trees were sold with a rotating color wheel that cast four colors onto its reflective tinsel branches.

Larry and Darrin Lazertran Ornaments

Materials

- 1 box Krebs Polar White glass ball ornaments (more if necessary)
- Christmas card clip art (page 124)
- 1 package Lazertran Paper (for glass and ceramics)
- Scissors
- Handheld hairdryer
- Color laser copier

Tree Trivia The Christmas tree dates back to a seventh century legend about a monk in Devonshire, England who used the triangle shape of the fir tree to represent the Holy Trinity. By the twelfth century, the tree was being hung from the ceiling... upside-down!

For a bewitching trick, try personalizing all your tree ornaments this year with a favorite image or graphic. Anything from childhood photos to old Christmas cards will do the job nicely.

1. Using the art on page 124 or another design of choice, have your image reduced to a size that will fit your ornament by using a laser copy machine at your local copy center. (We use Kinko's.)

2. Next, have the image repeated several times over on the same sheet of paper.

3. Copy master sheet onto Lazertran Paper (full instructions included with every package).

4. Use a scissors to trim each image down to size. Keep in mind that the less paper around the image, the easier to have it adhere to the curved surface of the glass ball.

5. Follow instructions on Lazertran package to remove image from paper backing and adhere it to glass ball.

6. Use the hot air from the hairdryer to smooth all the wrinkles out. This takes a bit of practice, but you'll get it!

Ornament Clusters

These clusters are a variation of the ones in the Candy Cane Christmas section, but with a different color scheme. Rather than red and silver balls, use pink, blue, green, and silver to go along with the other decorations in this section.

Materials

- Several packages plastic ornaments (pink, blue, green, and silver in various shapes and sizes)
- Hot glue gun and glue sticks

1. Use hot glue to affix plastic ornaments to each other into large clusters, as shown in photo below. Vary ornament sizes.

2. You may want to start with one "core" ornament, such as the long, thin one shown here (2a), and glue smaller balls to it, as shown (2b). Keep in mind that each cluster may look different.

3. Let dry and hang as desired.

Decorating for Christmas

Space Balls

These plastic ornaments that look like glass are a breeze to make just by adding dots of paint that look a bit "spiky" when dry.

Materials

- 12 silver glass Christmas balls by Krebs (or color of choice)
- 1 each Polymark Dimensional Paint Pen
  - Pink
  - Pale green
  - Light blue

1. Hold ornament by the loop hanger and squeeze tiny globules from Polymark Paint Pens at random about the ball.
2. Pull Paint Pen outward each time to form tiny peaks.
3. Repeat steps 1 and 2 with each color until your ornament is covered with different colored globules, as shown bottom left.
4. To dry, hook a long metal ornament hanger to top loop of ball, place heavy mugs or cups with handles upside-down near the edge of a shelf, and hook the hanger to the cup handle allowing the ornaments to dangle freely, as shown at left.

Tree Trivia — Tinsel isn't exactly a new thing. It dates back to around 1610 and was made originally of real silver. In fact, it was still being made of silver well into the 20th century. We bet it was difficult to polish that!

Poodle Tree-Skirt

Who says all poodle skirts have to be worn by people? We think this one makes a perfect retro tree skirt. Appliquéd felt was big for Christmas decorations in the 1950s and '60s and the following is our version of some festive felt frillys!

For skirt top and petticoat:

1. For the skirt top, cut out a 50"-diameter circle from the light blue felt.

2. For the petticoat, repeat step 1 using the white felt and adding 5" for a circle with a 60" diameter.

3. Using scallop pattern on page 110 as a guide, draw on the backside of the white felt petticoat piece with a pencil and then cut scallop edging around the petticoat piece.

Materials

- 1½ yards 72"-wide light blue felt
- 1½ yards 72"-wide white felt
- 8 large LaVogue Pink Poodle Iron-on Appliqués
- 9" x 12 " pink felt piece
- 9" x 12 " dark green felt piece
- 9" x 12 " light green felt piece
- 9" x 12 " red felt piece
- 2 packages Therm O Web HeatnBond Iron-On Adhesive
- 1 package silver sequin snowflakes
- 1 package each pink, blue, and green star-shaped rhinestones
- Circle hole punch
- Diamond hole punch
- Sewing machine and thread
- Scissors or rotary cutter
- White glue
- Straight pins
- Iron
- Marker
- Pencil
- Patterns (pages 108-110)

La Vogue Pink Poodle Iron-on Appliqués.

4. Use hole punches to create a pattern on the edge of felt petticoat either as shown at right, or in your own design.

5. Center skirt on top of petticoat, pin, and machine stitch together ½" from edge of blue skirt.

6. Fold skirt into fourths, mark center with a pin, and then cut 2" off of point to create the hole for the tree trunk.

7. Open skirt once so it is still folded in half and then cut along fold line from center to one edge to form skirt opening.

8. Machine stitch along all cut edges.

For decorative accents:

1. Iron all felt squares to HeatnBond adhesive.

2. Using the patterns on pages 108-109, cut out the following:
- One sleigh, one sleigh runner, one large package, and one small package from pink felt.
- One tree, one medium package, and one small package from dark green felt.
- One tree and one medium package from light green felt.
- One large package from red felt.

3. Using the package patterns, cut contrasting rectangles of felt and iron to packages leaving a center "ribbon" showing.

4. Cut small ½" x 1" pieces from red felt. Iron to pink sleigh runner at a slight angle. Trim away excess red felt on either side of runner. This forms candy cane-like stripe, as shown at right.

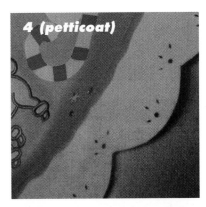

4 (petticoat)

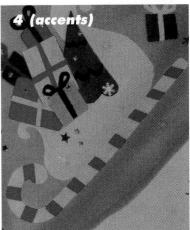

4 (accents)

6

5. Cut the scallop shapes from the light green tree piece and iron to dark green tree so scallops show between.

6. With skirt opening in back, iron sleigh and runner in place onto skirt using photo at left as a guide.

7. Arrange tree and packages in sleigh. When you are satisfied with their location, iron in place.

8. Iron poodles in pairs, slightly overlapping each other, starting 1" from front of runner. Place next set about 1½" in front of those, lining them up nose to tail, as shown bottom left.

9. Use white glue to dot silver sequin snowflakes and rhinestone stars about the sleigh and poodles. Let dry before use.

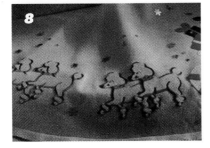

8

Silver-wrapped gifts-to-go! Just as we suggested in the Candy Cane Christmas section, let your decorating theme extend to your gift-wrap, bows, tags, and ribbons.

Retro-Table

Continue your jaunt back to the 50s by bringing the retro feel to your dining experience. It is simple to set a retro-table with embellishments to each table setting.

Retro Café Ware and Stemware

Materials

- 1 set white Café Ware dinner service for four by Culinary Arts
- Vintage clip art, drawing, Christmas card, or photo (Ours is on page 124.)
- Lazertran Paper (for glass and ceramics)
- 4 clear glass stemware

1. Wash and dry all dishes.

2. Have image sized to fit dish, cup, or salad plate at your local copy center, like Kinko's.

3. Have image transferred in onto Lazertran Paper.

4. Bake onto dishware according to package instructions on Lazertran Paper package.

Nothing quite creates that "diner" flair as much as diner place settings. Old-fashioned white diner tableware is readily available at many places that sell dishes. We found ours at a nationwide chain called Linens N' Things. With the addition of Christmas designs, you're sure to set the best table this side of Riverdale High!

Apply your favorite holiday image to the outside of the stemware using the Lazertran method.

Noël Note:

Even after Lazertran images have been baked on, they can usually be removed with careful scraping and washing; therefore, we do not recommend eating off of them. We suggest you serve dinner on a clear plate set on top of the design.

Vanilla Shakes with Peppermint Cream

What good are retro-looking glasses if you don't have something retro to put inside? Milkshakes to the rescue!

Materials

Milkshake Ingredients (serves four)
- ½-gallon vanilla ice cream
- ½-gallon whole milk
- 1 tsp. vanilla extract
- Electric blender
- Ice cream scoop

Topping Ingredients
- 1 pint heavy whipping cream
- Red food coloring
- 2 Tbs. peppermint extract
- 2 c. powdered sugar
- Electric beater
- 4 maraschino cherries

OK, let's get to blending! Kasey always wanted to be an Andrews Sister.

1. Put four large scoops vanilla ice cream into blender.

2. Fill with milk just to top of ice cream.

3. Add vanilla extract and blend until smooth.

4. In a mixing bowl, whip cream with beater until it starts to thicken. Slowly add powdered sugar to taste and beat until soft peaks begin to form.

5. Add peppermint extract and a few drops of red food coloring. Whip just until stiff.

6. Pour milkshakes into stemware.

7. Top with a dollop of peppermint whipped cream and garnish with cherry and candy cane to stir. Serve with long-handled spoon and a Poodle Pad (next page).

Poodle Pads

Made to match the Poodle Tree Skirt (even down to their little felt petticoats), these felt drink mats are ideal for serving. They won't fall off the bottom of your stemware and will protect your tables from unsightly water rings.

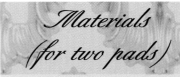

Materials (for two pads)

- 9" x 12" light blue felt piece
- 9" x 12" white felt piece
- 2 small LaVogue Pink Poodle Iron-on Appliqués
- Diamond-shaped hole punch
- Round hole punch
- Scissors or rotary cutter
- Iron
- Sewing machine and thread
- Patterns (page 111)

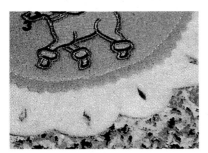

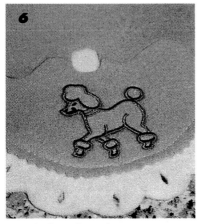

Detail of Poodle Pad.

1. Cut out light blue felt top and white felt petticoat using patterns found on page 111.
2. Cut "S" slit in light blue top as shown on pattern, to accommodate the base of the stemware.
3. Use hole punches to add decorative design in white petticoat, as shown at left.
4. Iron poodle onto blue top.
5. Center light blue top over petticoat and machine stitch around perimeter of light blue.
6. Nestle glass stemware bottom into slit prior to serving.

Poodle Placemats

Instead of a whole tablecloth, these placemats are perfect for a rather retro dining experience.

Materials (for four placemats)

- ½-yard 72"-wide light blue felt
- ½-yard 72"-wide pink felt
- Starburst pattern (page 110)
- Pinking shears
- Sewing machine and thread

1. With pinking shears, cut four 18" x 12" rectangles from the light blue felt.

2. Again with pinking shears, cut four 16" x 10" rectangles from pink felt.

3. Center pink rectangle on top of blue and topstitch 1" from pink edge.

4. Have your local copy store laser copy the starburst design onto opposite corners of the pink rectangle, as shown below.

Decorating for Christmas

Poodle Stockings

If you have got a poodle skirt (for the tree, that is) you better have some poodle socks to go with it.

Materials (for each)

- ¼-yard 36"-wide light blue felt
- ¼-yard 36"-wide white felt
- 1 large LaVogue Pink Poodle Iron-on Appliqué
- Diamond-shaped hole punch
- Round hole punch
- 1 package silver sequin snowflakes
- 1 package each blue, green, and pink rhinestone stars
- Sewing machine and thread
- 12" all-purpose white cotton string
- Pinking shears
- White glue
- Iron
- Patterns (pages 105-107)

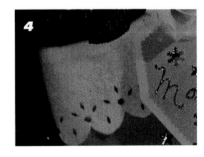

1. Using pattern on pages 106-107, cut two stocking sides from light blue felt.

2. Using pattern on page 105, cut one stocking topper from white felt.

3. Using ½" seam allowance, topstitch stocking sides together, leaving top open, and trim outside edges with pinking shears.

4. Use fabric punches to create design as shown at right, or in a different design as desired, in white felt topper's scalloped edge.

5. Stitch back seam of felt topper. Turn right-side out.

6. Place felt topper *inside* stocking, matching up raw edges on top. Be sure to begin and end topper seam on *calf* side of stocking. Stitch around top.

7. Pull topper straight up and out of stocking. Turn felt topper down over outside of stocking. Be careful not to pull too hard on the punched out holes as the felt can stretch or tear easily.

8. Iron poodle to front of stocking.

9. To hang stocking, make a loop by cutting a 1½" x 7" strip of light blue felt and a 12" length of string. Knot one end of string. Fold felt lengthwise, sandwiching string inside.

10. Machine stitch felt across knotted string end and along 7" side. Remove from machine and pull string through the felt turning loop right-side out as you go.

11. Cut string off and whipstitch loop inside stocking at calf seam.

12. Use white glue to affix silver sequin snowflakes and colored rhinestones on stocking. Don't forget to iron on that poodle, too.

Stocking Corsages

Embellish your Poodle Stockings and make sure everyone knows which is his or hers by adding these pretty nametag corsages.

Materials (for each)

- 3 silk roses or Christmas flowers of choice
- 1 berry spray
- Green floral tape
- 1 sheet bright green cardstock
- 1 sheet blue cardstock
- Polymark Silver Glitter Paint Pen
- 1 package silver sequin snowflakes
- 1 package each rhinestone stars in green, pink, and blue
- Double-sided sticky tape
- Small LaVogue Pink Poodle Iron-on Appliqué (or Christmas appliqué of choice)
- White glue
- Round hole punch
- Hot glue gun and glue sticks
- Patterns (page 112)

1. Wrap three roses and berry spray together with floral tape, as shown below left.

2. Cut two "tags" from cardstock using patterns, page 112, and tape together.

3. Hot glue poodle appliqué in place. Do not iron on as the heat can discolor some paper.

4. Write stocking recipients name on tag with Polymark Silver Glitter Paint Pen, as shown below.

5. Add sequin snowflakes and rhinestone stars using white glue.

6. Use hole punch to put a hole in top of tag.

7. Slip wrapped ends of roses through hole in tag and tuck stems into top of stocking.

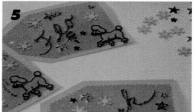

His and Hers Poodle Pocket Aprons

You certainly can't put together that retro Christmas meal in your poodle-packed home without decorating yourself to match. These aprons are not only perfect for getting you into that vintage Christmas spirit, but they also keep those nice holiday clothes clean when you are pulling the ham from the oven.

Materials (for hers)

- 1 yard 60"-wide light blue baby cord fabric
- 2 yards gathered white lace trim
- 1 large LaVogue Pink Poodle Iron-on Appliqué
- 1 package light blue single-fold bias tape
- Scissors
- Straight pins
- Iron
- Patterns (pages 113-114)

1. Fold fabric lengthwise and cut two strips from selvedge edges 9" wide by 60" long.
2. Cut apron on fold of remaining fabric using the pattern on page 113.
3. Using the pattern on page 114, cut pocket from remaining fabric.
4. Topstitch lace around apron edge with zigzag stitch.
5. Fold top of pocket down twice, ¾" each time, and press.
6. Iron on poodle (or Christmas appliqué of choice) to center of pocket.
7. Topstitch pocket to apron using a zigzag stitch.
8. Using a straight stitch, topstitch bias tape (on both sides) around raw edges of lace and pocket. Be sure to fold the bias tape under at the top of each pocket side.
9. Fold and pin the four apron pleats at waist and topstitch to hold. Set apron aside.
10. Stitch ties short-end to short-end creating a 9" x 120" strip.
11. Fold ties lengthwise with right sides together and pin at center seam. Measure 9" out from center and pin again. Repeat on other side.
12. Stitch ties from one outer pin to end, tapering end to a point. Repeat on other side, leaving a center opening in ties to accommodate width of apron including lace edge.
13. Trim away excess fabric at curved ends.
14. Turn ties right-side out and press flat, making sure raw edges of opening are also turned to the inside.
15. Insert top of apron into opening and pin to hold in place.
16. Topstitch ¼" around entire length of apron ties securing apron at same time.

Materials (for his)

- Pre-made 100% cotton all white chef apron
- Clip art, photo, or drawing of choice
- Iron

1. Have heat press transfer made of clip art made at your local copy center. Be sure and enlarge and *reverse print* image if needed.
2. Iron transfer to apron.

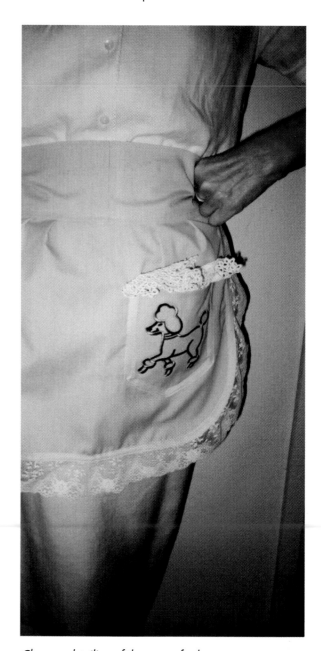

Close-up detailing of the apron for her.

Wretro Wreath

This wreath can hang in another room, hallway, or even on a door to help carry your retro theme into another area of your home. It is quick, easy, and oh-so-trendy!

Materials

- 1 plastic silver spire
- 1 pink "grape-like" cluster
- 3 large glass-like light blue plastic ornaments
- 4 large glass-like chartreuse plastic ornaments
- 2 medium glass-like silver plastic ornaments
- 14" straw wreath
- 1 package (25 feet) silver tinsel garland
- 2 14" silver tinsel branches
- 4 10" silver tinsel branches
- Greening pins
- Florist tape
- Hot glue gun and glue sticks

Noël Note:

We used branches from the back of our silver tree for the wreath. However, if you have used all of your branches, silver pine sprays are readily available at craft stores during the holidays. If not, get industrious and wrap lengths of sturdy florist wire with more tinsel garland and bend together to form branches!

1. Wrap entire wreath with tinsel garland as shown below until no straw shows. Secure both ends with the "U" shaped greening pins.
2. Place two short silver branches on top of one long silver branch. Wrap ends together with florist tape.
3. Use greening pins to hold the branches to the bottom of wreath.
4. Repeat steps 2 and 3 for opposite side.
5. Hot glue ornaments into a cluster and secure to wreath with greening pins at center bottom where branch ends meet, as shown.

Retro Serving Tray

Here's a fun way to give those scratched and seemingly worthless old vinyl records another spin. This serving tray is just groovy for holding everything from appetizers and desserts to votive candles.

Materials

- Tiered dessert stand
- 45 rpm record
- 78 rpm record
- Several votive candles with glass holders to match your color scheme

Noël Note:

Be sure to set the candles near the edge of the records so that the flames will not melt the record above.

1. Gently clean the records and let dry.
2. Unscrew china plates from dessert tier and replace with one 45 rpm record in top tier and a 78 rpm in the bottom tier.
3. Arrange votive candles decoratively on the stand, or use to display appetizers or desserts.

After our trip down Memory Lane, Kasey relaxes with a cup o' joe at Ed DeBevic's restaurant in Beverly Hills. Our many thanks to Peter (aka "Doc") for allowing us to take the photographs for this section in his diner. For more information on this fine eating establishment, see Resources, page 126.

A Sweet Deal

Add that same clip art, favorite photo, or Christmas card to the sides of those old-fashioned glass candy jars. We found ours at a local Goodwill store for a dollar! One thing to keep in mind, the images from the Lazertran Paper tend to be a bit faint on clear glass, so a white paper liner or marshmallows waiting to be toasted make a great backdrop inside the jars.

Candy in the Straws

Those old-fashioned soda fountain straw dispensers don't have to hold only straws. (We've been known to put spaghetti in ours.) Fill one with candy canes for a real retro treat. We used the same vintage design and Lazertran Paper to decorate our dispenser and lined the inside with a piece of white poster board cut to fit so the design would show up better.

Timeless Treasures

You don't have to eat in a diner to make your table look like you've stepped into one. Vintage-looking diner pieces such as this napkin holder and the salt-and-pepper shakers (above left) are readily available at many nationwide chain stores, such as Linens N' Things. And don't forget those great trinkets from the past (above right) to add that final touch of class!

Metallic Mantle

Make your mantle shimmer by pulling together the Wretro Wreath, candlesticks (explained below), and a vase (made by inserting a few silver branches into a crystal vase and embellishing with an ornament cluster). Sprinkle in something silver (like our deer) and finish with a few votive candles in coordinating colors. What a fun and festive feel!

Old Flame

A lack of taper candles? No problem, turn an ornament cluster over and secure it to a crystal candlestick with earthquake putty or museum wax. Place a few more ornament clusters about the shelf, mantle or centerpiece for an instant holiday look that goes up quickly and packs away for future use even faster.

An Easter Christmas

This green glass poodle nestled in leftover pink Easter grass fits right in with the retro feel of this chapter. Try using the Easter grass instead of angel hair or icicles as tree filler. Don't be afraid to mix holidays!

Decorating for Christmas

Country Cabin Christmas

The old-fashioned mail keeper is available from Tender Heart Treasures (Resources , page 127).

Got cabin fever? Then why not decorate to make yourself feel as though you are resting up in the Northwoods? The projects in this section create the ambience that says the spirit of Christmas has come in from the woods to warm his toes and rest his weary self.

Natural Garland

A warm winter welcome greets you the moment you step through the front door of the Newbury House, an early 1800s pioneer cabin. No need buying expensive garland from a nursery, it is actually quite easy to make. And what better way to hold up a garland of fresh greens over the door than two jolly bear towel rings? We used these same resin bear towel rings (any decorative towel ring will do) both outside and in, as you will see on the following pages.

Materials

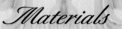

- Several small clippings of evergreens*
- Florist wire on a roll
- Pre-made berry garland**

*We used two different types of pine: one short needle and one long along with several clippings of a blue-green fitzer-type bush, but any evergreen will do. Use whatever type(s) of evergreen that are indigenous to your area.

**This is optional, but the garland must be based on a wire, and you will find that the red berries can lend a wonderful *Christmasy* feel.

1. Unroll the berry garland, straightening it out as you go.
2. Gather two or three clippings (one of each if using several different types of evergreen) and wrap ends tightly with florist wire, as shown at left.
3. Add berry garland to the very end of the evergreens and continue to wrap the wire around ends of the entire grouping, as shown at left.
4. Gather another set of clippings and repeat, overlapping the ends of the previous set of clippings by 2" or 3".
5. Continue in this manner until reaching the center. Stop here and begin again starting at the other end. This way, all the boughs will drape nicely. Most often a store-bought garland will only go one way. If you do use a store-bought one, cut it in half and wire the center back together so the boughs drape nicely down each side.
6. Pull red berries up through greenery.

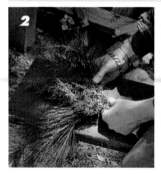

Noël Note:

Real berries tend to turn black and wither quickly, especially when put in water. Artificial ones, however, will be just as bright and pretty in your arrangements long after the real greenery has become dry, brittle and better suited for kindling!

Bucks Stop Here

Stepping around to the back of the cabin, we find another reminder that Santa and his flying friends are always welcome.

Materials

- 6" x 24" weathered wooden plank
- Flat wooden moose cut-out
- 1"-tall wooden letters (two T's, two H's, three E's, one B, one U, one C, one K, two S's, one O, one P, and one R)
- 5 black tea bags
- 2-oz. bottle red acrylic paint
- 2-oz. bottle black acrylic paint
- Spray bottle
- 18" of bailing wire
- Boiling pan and water
- Newspaper
- Paper plate or aluminum foil
- Paintbrush
- Hot glue gun and glue sticks
- Drill and ⅛" bit

1. Boil water and make a strong tea.

2. When cooled, place the dark tea solution into spray bottle.

3. Place letters outside on a piece of newspaper, making sure they are where they will get full sunlight. Spray five to six times a day with the dark tea solution over a period of five days, allowing letters to dry in between sprays.

4. Put a small amount of red and black acrylic paint next to each other on a plate (or piece of foil).

5. Using a dry brush, paint both colors simultaneously onto wooden moose. Paint with the grain and let red be your dominant color by using just a touch of black.

6. When letters are appropriately "stained," hot glue them and the moose to the board.

7. Use a drill to bore a hole on both right and left sides of the sign about 6" from top.

8. Run the bailing wire through each hole and bend ends to form handle.

9. For added embellishment, hang a few real carrots from a separate nail next to the sign as shown in the main project photo.

Close-up detail of sign.

Tree Trivia

The first decorated Christmas tree was in Latvia in 1510. Martin Luther is said to have first put candles on the tree to depict the stars that were shining the night Christ was born.

Dining For Two

"The table was set by the chimney with care..." Once inside this little cabin in the woods we find a table set with red and black buffalo plaid linens all ready to serve its Christmas Eve repast.

Log Cabin Centerpiece

What better tabletop centerpiece than a small version of our cabin home made from Lincoln Logs? What makes this little log cabin so perfect is the addition of small battery-operated Christmas lights and real snow on its roof. Real snow? Well, almost! There's a wonderful new product out called SnoWonder.

- Lincoln Log set
- 12"-square piece sturdy cardboard
- 1 roll aluminum foil
- SnoWonder
- Duct tape
- Spritzer bottle with water
- 2 battery-operated light strands
- Small bottle Rubber Cement
- 2 raw wood evergreen trees by Judy's Designs
- Scissors or rotary cutter

All you need is a little water and—voila—instant snow! It's even a bit cold to the touch.

Noël Note:

SnoWonder will slowly dry out over time, leaving you with just hard little lumps. Have no fear: a little spray of water and you will be back to volumes of snow. It can be saved from year to year and used over and over again.

1. Cover area of table to be used for centerpiece with foil and build cabin on top, omitting the green roof tiles found within the Lincoln Log set.

2. Place light strings inside cabins before adding roof. Be sure there is easy access to turn them on and off through a doorway.

3. Cut roof sides out of the 12" cardboard square by measuring the dimensions of the roof opening and trimming the cardboard to fit.

4. Cut the cardboard down the center and then tape roof sides together along that center cut so it conforms easily to the roof.

5. Cover rooftop with duct tape so no cardboard is exposed. Make sure cardboard roof is held in place by the notched ends of the red roof supports—duct tape side up, as shown below.

6. Brush liberal amount of rubber cement onto duct tape.

7. Sprinkle entire roof with SnoWonder powder, as shown below.

8. Spritz the roof with water carefully as shown so as not to *blow* the powder off the surface. The SnoWonder will immediately begin to expand.

9. Once the entire roof has been "watered" wait a few seconds and add more SnoWonder where it looks a bit bare. Don't forget to add the Lincoln Log chimney.

10. Add SnoWonder to the base of the cabin (on top of the foil). If too much foil shows through just fold under and pile on the snow.

Did You Know?

The son of famed architect Frank Lloyd Wright first introduced Lincoln Logs to the public in 1916.

Grapevine Wreath Chargers and Place Cards

The black plates and mugs, while not exactly the Christmas color of choice, fit perfectly with the rustic homespun look of the buffalo plaid linens—especially when set atop a grapevine wreath plate charger. These plates, by Libby Glassware are called Java Lava.

Mimicking the grapevine wreath charger is a tiny grapevine wreath place card holder.

1. Line top half of double-boiler with foil (for easy clean up).

2. Spread more foil on the counter nearby.

3. Add water to bottom half of double boiler and bring to boil. Turn down to a simmer.

4. Add paraffin to foil-lined top half and allow it to melt over hot water.

5. One at a time, dip berries and leaves in melted paraffin and then into cool water, as shown (5a, 5b). Repeat this dipping process until leaves and berries begin to look "frosted."

6. Allow dipped leaves and berries to cool on foil.

7. On one of the longer green leaves, use the Sharpie marker to write the name of a guest.

8. Dip this leaf as well, but not so much as to obscure the name.

9. Hot glue leaves and berries to small grapevine wreath so the name leaf is clearly visible, as shown below right.

10. Set on top of or beside plate.

Materials

- 4" grapevine wreath (per guest)
- Various real leaves and berries
- Black Sharpie marker
- Double-boiler
- 1 roll aluminum foil
- Small pan with cold water
- 5"-square piece paraffin
- Hot glue gun and glue sticks

Woodland Cornucopia Napkin Holders

Hanging on the back of one's chair may be an unusual place to find a napkin, but when it's tucked inside these paper leaf-laden cornucopias, it seems as natural as the woods outside.

Materials (per cone)

- 8" cardboard doll cone
- 2 packages green Decorative Accents Paper Leaves
- 4" grapevine wreath
- 12" red berry pick
- Aileene's Stiffy
- Bowl
- Water
- Hot glue gun and glue sticks

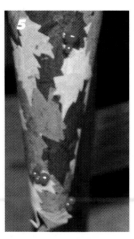

1. In a bowl, dilute a half-cup Aileene's Stiffy with half-cup water (enough for one cone).

2. Dip one paper leaf at a time in mixture, and starting at the bottom, smooth the leaves onto cone. Allow the bottom leaves to extend about ½" past bottom of cone.

3. Continue in same manner, slightly overlapping leaves as you work your way to the top of the cone. Allow to dry.

4. Hot glue wreath to top of cone.

5. Remove several berries from pick and hot glue around the body of the cone in groups of three, as shown at left.

6. Add berries from pick around wreath top, as shown in lower left photo.

7. Use rest of berries on wire to form handle. Nestle ends of berry wire into opposite sides of wreath, hot glue to hold.

8. Hang from back of chair and tuck napkin inside, as shown at left.

The Cabin Hearth

This cabin's flue is all ready for Santa and his crew. Draped with fresh greens from the forest outside, the rock chimney and hearth promote lots of good cheer with a few surprises of its own!

Reindeer Feedbag

And just why should Santa get all the goodies on his nocturnal rounds? It seems to us that there are eight tiny reindeer (maybe nine depending on the weather) doing an awful lot of work. We bet they could use a cookie or two themselves! Here's a feedbag made just for them—and any sneaky elves who might need a break while putting together that bicycle during the wee hours of Christmas morn!

Materials

- ½-yard burlap in natural color
- ½-yard thin clear plastic sheeting (used for table coverings)
- 1¼ yards large cotton cording
- 1" wooden letters (one F, two E's, one D, one B, one A, and one G)
- Flat wooden moose cut-out
- 5 black tea bags
- 2-oz. bottle red acrylic paint
- 2-oz. bottle black acrylic paint
- Spray bottle
- Boiling pan and water
- Newspaper
- Paper plate or aluminum foil
- Paintbrush
- Hot glue gun and glue sticks
- Scissors or rotary cutter
- Several straight sewing pins
- Thread to match burlap
- Sewing machine
- Iron

For the letters and moose:

1. Boil water and make a strong tea.

2. When cooled, place the dark tea solution into spray bottle.

3. Place letters outside on a piece of newspaper, making sure they are where they will get full sunlight. Spray five to six times a day with the dark tea solution over a period of five days, allowing letters to dry in between sprays.

4. Put a small amount of red and black acrylic paint next to each other on a plate (or piece of foil).

5. Using a dry brush, paint both colors simultaneously onto wooden moose. Paint with the grain and let red be your dominant color by using just a touch of black.

6. Let dry thoroughly.

For the bag:

1. Cut out two 16" x 24" rectangles of burlap.

2. Cut out two 16" x 18" rectangles from the plastic sheeting. Do not discard the tissue paper that comes on the plastic sheeting, as the paper will enable you to sew it on the machine.

3. Sandwich burlap between the plastic sheeting, making sure the tissue paper is on the outside of both sides. Align the bottom edge of tissue, plastic sheeting, and burlap, and pin to hold.

4. With ½" seam allowance, stitch through all layers around bottom and two sides. Remove tissue.

5. Turn the excess of burlap top down 1" and press with a steam iron.

6. Turn down burlap again to just cover the top of the plastic sheeting and press.

7. Stitch turned-down burlap top in place, making sure you catch the plastic as you go.

8. Go up 1½" from first stitch line and stitch around bag again to form casing.

Close-up of Reindeer Feed Bag.

9. Turn bag right-side out.

10. Fold bottom corners of bag in to meet each other. Stitch corner points together.

11. Reach inside bag and stitch corner points to center of bottom seam (much like a paper bag is glued together on the bottom). The bag should stand on this base.

12. Hot glue the tea stained letters and red stained moose in place on the bag.

13. Make a small opening in the casing on the outside center front of bag.

14. Knot both ends of cording so it won't fray and work it through the casing. Use cord to tie off bag.

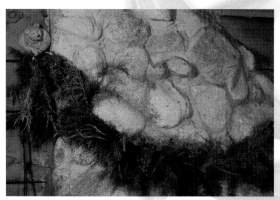
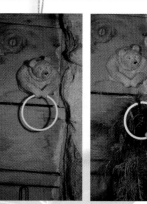

Grin and Bear It

Remember those friendly towel ring cubs outside that were holding up the Christmas garland over the cabin doorway? Well, they're from Tender Heart Treasures (Resources, page 127) and we have them hung all over the place, including hiding on either side of the chimney.

To put garland into towel ring, first remove ring from its holder, set swag inside ring and return to holder. These snapped easily into place; some towel rings, however, must be unscrewed from their holder and screwed back in. Either way, there are numerous types of towel rings available and they make fantastic garland holders.

These Boots Were Made for Decoratin'

Instead of the usual stockings, why not spray paint (using Design Master's Holiday Red) a couple of cast-off cowboy boots? These hold packages easily wrapped in brown paper grocery bags with bows of pinecones hot glued to their prettiest side.

An old teddy bear whose stuffing has found its way to the outside through a couple of worn seams watches intently over the hearth waiting to catch a glimpse of Santa and his merry band. We added the necktie to help tie the bear in with our color scheme.

The Country Hearth

Not only are the stockings hung by the chimney with care, but we've joined them with some Pennsylvania Dutch-like felt mittens. Photographed at the home of our good friends Amanda Fox and Lisa Wilke, this warm country parlor hearth is brimming over with happy Christmas ideas that are so easy to make.

Dutch Mittens

These frosty felt mittens can be used in a number of cool ways. One idea is to stick small branches inside them and place them in a clay pot for a lovely arrangement. Invite guests to "pick a mitten posy" to place their mug of hot chocolate on.

Or clothespin several to a vine and use as a homespun garland across a mantle or window as seen in the first photo of the hearth on the previous page. They can even be filled with small yummies.

Materials

- 4 mottled red 9" x 12" felt pieces
- 4 mottled green 9" x 12" felt pieces
- 4 stone-colored 9" x 12" felt pieces
- 1 skein black DMC embroidery floss
- Several ¾" wooden buttons
- 1 fabric paint pen each in white, black, and red
- 16" clay pot (optional)

- Various branches and vines (optional)
- 2 wooden clothespins (optional)
- Scissors or rotary cutter
- Sewing machine or hand needle and thread
- Hot glue gun and glue sticks
- Patterns (pages 115-116)

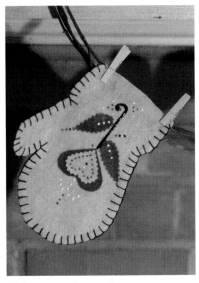

1. Using the pattern found on page 115, cut four mitten halves from each color felt.

2. Use patterns on page 116 to cut hearts, leaves, and flowers in the appropriate colors for each.

3. Machine stitch or blanket stitch by hand (instructions below) around perimeter of mitten, using a ¼" seam allowance.

4. Hot glue felt appliqués to the mittens.

5. Finish off by dotting paint from the nozzle of the pens in various patterns and designs around the appliqués.

Detail of both the green and stone-colored felt mittens shown above.

To blanket stitch: Bring needle and thread up through back to front about ½" from edge of felt. Re-enter again through back about ½" from first entry. Bring through to front. Before entering back again, catch thread so it will run along edge. Continue in this manner to end. Knot off.

The felt Dutch Mittens shown above in the clothesline homespun garland variation and at right as cozy coasters beneath mugs of hot chocolate and with the Iron Star Candlesticks, page 78.

Wood Topiary

This festive little miniature tree, which is made with several organic ingredients, allows you to bring a bit of the outdoors inside. It is the optimal way to enjoy nature in the midst of December without worrying about Jack Frost nipping at your nose while you admire the tree.

Materials

- 5" clay pot
- 1 block Floracraft Dry Foam
- 6"-long stick (1"-wide diameter)
- 12"-high three-dimensional wooden tree (6" across base)
- Patina Antiquing Kit by Modern Options
- 1 package reindeer moss
- Hot glue gun and glue sticks

1. Verdigris the wooden tree according to package instructions on patina kit. Set aside to dry.
2. Trim dry foam to fit snugly inside clay pot.
3. Hot glue foam in place.
4. Press one end of stick deep into foam, remove, fill hole with hot glue, and reinsert stick.
5. Be sure top of stick is level and hot glue wooden tree base to stick.
6. Cover Floracraft foam with the reindeer moss.

Moss Topiary

A simple variation of the Wood Topiary, this project is just a bit more colorful with its moss green and berry red color scheme.

Materials

- 5" clay pot
- 1 block Floracraft Dry Foam
- 12"-long stick (1"-wide diameter)
- 8" cardboard cone
- 1 package reindeer moss
- 2 picks artificial red berries
- 6 to 8 artificial green velvet leaves
- Hot glue gun and glue sticks

1. Hot glue reindeer moss to cardboard cones.

2. Nestle red berries and velvet leaves in moss, hot glue to hold in place, and set aside.

3. Trim dry foam to fit snugly inside clay pot.

4. Hot glue foam in place.

5. Press one end of stick deep into foam, remove, fill hole with hot glue, and reinsert stick.

6. Place the moss/cone trees over top of stick. It should balance there just fine without securing with glue.

7. Cover Floracraft foam with leftover reindeer moss.

Iron Star Candlesticks

These wrought-iron stars once adorned the outsides of old buildings and were a decorative means to show where strategic support beams ran. Today, these stars can be found by the dozens at flea markets and swap meets.

Materials

- Wrought-iron stars (any size)
- Wooden candle cups
- Instant Rust Kit by Modern Options
- 9" x 12" dark brown felt piece (makes two)
- Scissors or rotary cutter
- Hot glue gun and glue sticks
- 2 taper candles
- Red berries (optional)

1. "Rust" the wooden candle cups according to package instructions and allow them to dry.

2. Cut a felt star shape using the iron star as a guide.

3. Hot glue felt to bottom of star, trimming edges so they do not show.

4. Hot glue candle cups to center of iron star.

5. Insert candles in cups and light. Add red berries for display purposes, if you like.

Overall view of a Country Christmas mantle.

Reindeer Candleholder

Known for lighting the way, these Christmas reindeer are giving Rudolph a helping hoof in guiding Santa's sleigh. These vintage Gurley deer candles are far too precious to even consider burning (they can be found on eBay and in antique stores), but they still shine standing in the "snow" next to this hurricane lamp.

Materials

- Small plate
- Vintage Gurley brand deer candles
- Clear glass hurricane globe (to fit on plate)
- 1 can DAPtex Insulating Foam
- 1 tube Creative Beginnings Ultra Fine Blue Violet Diamond Dust Glitter
- 2"-square piece of cardboard
- Pillar candle

1. Place candle and hurricane globe in center of plate.

2. Use the DAPtex to obscure all traces of the plate. (It will wash off with a little soap and water when through.)

3. Embed a deer in the DAPtex while it is still wet and sprinkle with glitter.

4. Make small dollops of DAPtex to cover cardboard and embed more deer candles.

5. Sprinkle with glitter while DAPtex is still wet.

6. Use deer on cardboard to complement hurricane display, as shown in the project photo at left.

Homespun Cornucopias

Cornucopias to hang on the tree were a popular turn-of-the-century pastime to make. Here is a different and quick way to make them for today.

1. Roll cone in fabric starting in a corner. For the green one, we used two contrasting check fabrics—one as a lining.

2. Turn back the last edge at the top and hot glue fabric to hold in place.

3. To make bow, fray all edges of 3" x 9" fabric scrap and fold one-third over on top and one-third under on bottom.

4. Squeeze strip together in center and stitch to hold.

5. Wrap center area with another 2" x 4" scrap of same fabric for "knot." Stitch knot in place.

6. Hot glue bow to front flap of cornucopia.

7. Hot glue leaf-shaped button to the cornucopia.

8. Fill with small decorations, such as the stuffed bears we used in ours.

Noël Note:

The back point formed from a corner of the fabric can easily be made with a buttonhole to hang the cornucopias but we decided to set ours in a glass on top of the fireplace mantle. It leaves more room for stockings that need filling!

Materials (per cone)

- 2 cardboard 8" cones (for doll/angel bodies)
- 10" x 12" scrap of woven fabric
- 5" x 9" scrap of woven fabric
- 2 leaf-shaped buttons or trims of choice
- Hot glue gun and glue sticks
- Needle and thread

Honey Bear Lights and Log Cabin Lights

These projects show just how easy it is to recycle honey and syrup containers into decorative accents for your home. Each finished piece gives off a warm glow perfect for warming hearts on those cold winter nights.

Materials

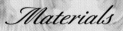

- 1 sheet
  2' x 3' x ¼" pegboard
- 12½"-long piece of 2" x 3" wood
- 26"-long piece of 1" x 3" wood
- 1 package lamp kit for a bottle
- 25-watt bulb (color of choice; we used yellow.)
- 4 wooden 1" balls
- 12 finishing nails
- 1 tube Creative Beginnings Ultra Fine Blue Violet Diamond Dust Glitter
- 5 Log Cabin Syrup bottles (in various sizes)
- 5 plastic honey bear bottles (in various sizes)
- 2 pair old colored socks

- Delta Air-Dry Permenamel Transparent Glass Paint
  - 2 bottles Amber
  - 2 bottles Yellow
- Gray paint by Scribbles
- Black Sharpie pen
- 1 can DAPtex Insulating Foam
- 1 package moss
- ¼-yard green or brown felt
- Handsaw
- Several assorted small twigs
- Drill with 1" and 1⅜" bits
- Sewing machine
- Needle and thread to match sock colors
- Hot glue gun and glue sticks
- Newspaper
- Dish soap and water

For the light box:
1. With saw, cut a rectangle of pegboard 12½" x 9¼" for bottom of box.
2. Cut two rectangles that are 1" bigger on all sides for tops. Set aside.
3. Reserve 2" x 3" wood piece for back of base.
4. Saw 1" x 3" wood piece into two 6¾" lengths, leaving one 12½" length. These are the two sides and front of box.
5. Nail box frame together with side pieces *inside* of front and back pieces.

6. Drill a 1⅜" hole through back of box to accommodate light fixture, as shown at right.

7. Nail pegboard to bottom of frame.

8. Referring to the photo for assistance, insert fixture and add bulb.

9. Hot glue little ball feet on each corner of bottom, as shown.

10. Slice felt down the middle and gather in pleats on the sewing machine.

11. Hot glue felt ruffle around outside of box and set box aside.

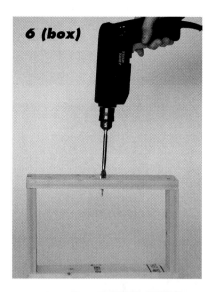

6 (box)

For the bears:

1. Drain honey into another bottle and wash bear bottles thoroughly.

2. When dry, squirt enough yellow paint inside bottle to fill ½" and swirl paint around inside bear until completely coated. Set bear upside-down on newspaper to drain and dry.

3. Use the Sharpie to draw on features, as shown below right.

4. Cut caps and scarves from old socks.

5. Gather the tops of the socks with needle and thread to form knit caps. It's fun to wrap the scarves around their noses and mouth 'cause, baby, it's cold outside!

6. Drill a 1" hole in the pegboard top where you wish each bear to sit.

7. Hot glue bear over hole and surround with DAPtex snow.

8. Sprinkle with Diamond Dust Glitter while DAPtex is still wet. Allow to dry.

9. Set decorated pegboard on top of light box and flip the switch for a wonderful glow.

8 (box)

For the cabins:

1. Empty, wash, and paint the bottles amber as done to bear bottles.

2. When dry; carefully saw off the screw top part of each bottle, as shown below.

3. Paint the chinking between the "logs" using the gray paint by Scribbles, as shown. Be sure to paint the chimney top as well.

4. Add DAPtex "snow" to roofs and chimney tops, as shown below.

5. While DAPtex is still wet, sprinkle with copious amounts of Diamond Dust Glitter.

6. When dry, hot glue doors and windows made from twigs and leaves to the fronts of the cabins. Add small squirts of DAPtex snow to door and window frames.

7. Drill 1" holes in the pegboard top for each cabin.

8. Hot glue cabins in place.

9. Add moss pathways and DAPtex snow to pegboard.

10. When dry, place rear-decorated pegboard on top of light box with cabin pegboard first.

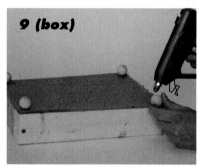

9 (box)

3 (bears)

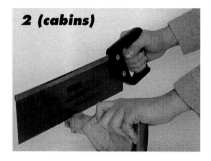

2 (cabins)

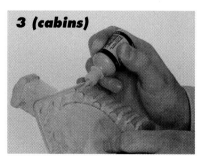

3 (cabins)

4 (cabins)

Good Little Soldiers

Remember sitting at "the kids' table" when you were young? And as one got older, the "dreaded" kids' table loomed larger! So, instead of making it a cast-off place so the adults can have their peace, try turning this special eating area into a place that Grandma just may be a little jealous of.

The Table

Soldier Boy Table Topper

Square table toppers are fairly quick and easy to make and can be made of any fabric, including a Christmas print. Since many fabrics come 60" wide, our table topper is an easy 56"-square finished. Toppers can be used alone or paired with a floor-length cloth on a round, square, or rectangular table.

Materials

- 1⅔ yards 60"-wide white cotton sailcloth
- Soldier Boy clip art (page 125)
- Lazertran Paper
- Iron
- Straight pins
- Sewing machine and thread

1. Wash and dry fabric.

2. Fold and iron the fabric edges down 1" and then 1" again, holding hem in place with pins as needed.

3. Machine stitch hem ⅞" from edge of table topper.

4. Using the Soldier Boy clip art found on page 125, go to your local copy center and have both the red and blue soldier boys enlarged 200% on the color copier to fill an 8½" x 11" sheet of paper.

5. Next, make laser copies of each (two red, two blue) onto the Lazertran Paper.

6. With iron, press images onto alternating corners of the cloth.

Mark readies the kids' table for the onslaught of Christmas Eve laughter and hijinks.

Decorating for Christmas

Front and Center

Since you never know when the kids might get a little too rowdy at Christmas, we decided on a cute but inexpensive blue vase centerpiece. It only looks like glass, but is actually plastic. Kasey filled it with red, blue, and green berries and red-and blue-striped candy canes to complement the color scheme and let the Candlestick Party Favors, and matching soldier ornaments serve as decoration.

Good Little Soldiers

Candlestick Party Favors

At the turn of the 1900s and well into the '30s and '40s, party-goers would make what was called a "Jack Horner Pie," which was a tabletop centerpiece decoration filled with all kinds of goodies. It was a sitting piñata of sorts and was always disguised as part of the décor. Sometimes these "pies" would be made for individual guests as we have done here by hiding a treasured trinket in a chamber stick.

Materials (per favor)

- Toilet paper cardboard tube
- 1 Package red tissue paper
- 5" beveled-edge wooden circle
- 1½" flat wood snowflake
- 1 tube Creative Beginnings Ultra Fine Green Diamond Dust Glitter
- 2-oz. bottle Cobalt Blue #20411 Apple Barrel Colors by Plaid
- 2-oz. bottle yellow acrylic paint by Plaid
- White acrylic paint pen by Plaid
- 1"-wide paintbrush
- Handsaw
- 1½" wooden teardrop shape
- PEZ Candy Dispenser or other small favor
- Hot glue gun and glue sticks

Decorating for Christmas

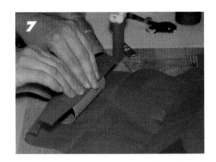

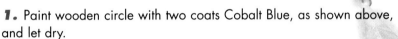

Close-up detailing of one of our finished Candlestick Party Favors.

1. Paint wooden circle with two coats Cobalt Blue, as shown above, and let dry.

2. Paint snowflake with two coats white paint, sprinkle with glitter while still wet, and let dry.

3. Paint teardrop with yellow paint, sprinkle with glitter while wet, and allow to dry.

4. Saw notch in one side of wooden circle, as shown, but do not saw all the way through.

5. Insert snowflake into notch and secure with hot glue, as shown.

6. When glue is dry, cover "seam" with more white acrylic paint and glitter. Set aside to dry.

7. Roll toilet paper tube in red tissue, as shown, and tuck tissue inside one end, leaving other end open.

8. Hot glue bottom of tube with tissue tucked inside to middle of blue wooden circle, as shown.

9. Slip PEZ Candy Dispenser or other favors into tube. Tuck tissue inside to close.

10. Hot glue wooden "flame" standing on top, as shown.

11. Drip hot glue around top of "candle" to simulate melting wax (11a) and sprinkle with glitter while still warm (11b).

Bailey, Michael, Varsha and Christopher can easily wait for dinner while tearing into their candle favors looking for the hidden treasures inside.

Bailey and Varsha play tug-o-war while waiting for dinner. After all those Candy Canes, who can eat?

Decorating for Christmas

Soldier Boy Chair Pads

Using chair pads to decorate your existing chairs at the table is another great way to add another dash of holiday fun to the party without taking too much time, effort, or expense. These pads carry the same motif as the tablecloth and curtains, but you can experiment with something that is slightly different as long as the overall theme of your table is maintained.

1. With serrated knife, cut foam into circle (or square) using chair seat as a guide. This will be your base.

2. Cut two white sailcloth circles, each 1½" wider than the foam base.

3. Cut a 3"-wide strip from the checked fabric, long enough to encircle the foam base. If the 45" is not long enough, cut more and machine piece together end-to-end.

4. Cut two 5" x 45" strips from remaining checked fabric.

5. Sew 5"-wide strips together end-to-end.

6. Press seam open with iron, fold right-side out along entire 90" strip, and then press flat.

7. Hand- or machine-gather 90" strip into a ruffle to fit around edge of sailcloth and set aside.

8. Take the top sailcloth circle to your local copy center and have them enlarge and print the Soldier Boy design, page 125, onto the center of the fabric.

9. With right sides together, line up raw edges of top circle, ruffle, and checked side-piece, pin, and stitch, leaving ½" seam allowance. Stitch checked-edge piece ends closed. Trim away all excess as needed.

10. With right sides together, pin bottom sailcloth piece to checkered-edge piece and stitch three-quarters of the way around.

11. Turn right-side out and insert foam. Smooth flat.

12. Hand-stitch the rest of seam closed.

Materials (per chair pad)

- ½-yard white sailcloth
- ½-yard 45"-wide red or blue checked fabric
- 2"-thick foam cushion to fit chair seat (circle or square)
- Soldier Boy clip art (page 125) or other artwork of choice
- Serrated kitchen knife
- Sewing machine and thread
- Iron
- Scissors or rotary cutter
- Several straight pins

Soldier Boy Pillows

Toss pillows are a great way to supplement your holiday decorating since all you really need to make are the covers. The inserts can be the sofa pillows that normally rest on your couch. You just need to dress them up for the holidays, or if you prefer, make some from scratch as we did with ours here.

Materials (per pillow)

- ½-yard white sailcloth
- ½-yard 45"-wide red or blue checked fabric
- Soldier Boy clip art (page 125) or other artwork of choice
- 16" square Polyfil pillow insert
- Sewing machine and thread
- Scissors or rotary cutter
- Iron

Noël Note:

Be sure all corners of pillow are machine-stitched down, leaving the opening in the bottom only about 9" to 10".

Bailey decided the throw pillows would look great in her room, so away they went!

1. Cut two 18" squares from the white sailcloth.
2. Cut three 6" x 45" strips from the checked fabric.
3. Stitch each strip end-to-end, forming one 6" x 135" piece.
4. Press open seam with iron, fold with right sides out, and press flat.
5. Machine- or hand-gather strip into ruffle, long enough to encircle edges of sailcloth square and set aside.
6. Take the Soldier Boy clip art on page 125 to your local copy center (like Kinko's Copy Center) and have it enlarged and transferred to the center of one 18" square.
7. With right sides together, align raw edges of top, ruffle, and bottom.
8. Pin and stitch, starting at bottom of pillow. Leave bottom edge open.
9. Turn pillow right-side out, insert pillow form, and handstitch the rest of seam closed.

Soldier Boy Café Curtains and Valance

Materials

- 6 yards 36"-wide muslin*
- 2 yards red-and-white striped fabric
- Soldier Boy clip art (page 125), or other artwork of choice
- Sewing machine and thread
- Measuring tape
- Scissors or rotary cutter
- Iron

*Amount of muslin will vary depending on size of window. For a 6- x 5-foot window, we needed 6 yards.

The Soldier Boy (or other image) can be readily applied to pre-made curtains or you can make your own curtains as in the instructions here. Go ahead and give it a try. The only skills needed are cutting and sewing a straight line. We used 36"-wide muslin for our curtains. Wash and iron all fabrics according to directions on bolt before sewing.

For café curtains:

1. Measure width of your window and double that figure.

2. For café curtains, rod should be positioned just slightly higher than halfway up window. Measure from rod to sill and add 12".

3. Cut a piece of muslin according to your measurements in step 2. Cut in half at center leaving two panels.

4. Turn bottom of one panel up 6" and press. Turn up 6" again and press.

5. Topstitch hem ¼" from top edge.

6. Turn sides under ½" twice. Press and topstitch.

7. Repeat steps 4 through 6 for other panel.

For header:

1. For header with ruffle, measure around rod and add 5".

2. Cut strips of red-and-white striped fabric to equal measurement in step 1 of this section by length of each panel top. (If it takes more than one strip to equal your measurement, stitch end-to-end with right sides together and press seams open flat.)

3. With right sides together, stitch striped fabric to top of curtain panel with a ½" seam allowance.

4. Press seam flat.

5. Turn raw edge of striped fabric down ½" and press.

6. Fold striped fabric lengthwise to meet first seam, topstitch, and press fold.

7. Stitch along length of striped fabric again, forming a pocket large enough to accommodate your rod.

8. Repeat steps 3 through 7 for other panel.

For valance:

1. Determine the drop measurement. The drop of the finished valance should equal about one-quarter the height of the window.

2. Cut strips of muslin double the length of your window by the drop measurement plus 3" (drop measurement x 2 + 3 = strip length).

3. Stitch strips end-to-end, if needed.

4. Press seams open flat.

5. Beginning with bottom hem, turn up 1" and press. Then turn up 1" again, press, and topstitch ¼" from top of hem edge.

6. The top header is be made the same as the curtain panel header, so follow those instructions to complete the valance.

Noël Note:

When pressing the hem in the panels, it's a good idea to measure every so often to make sure the hem is staying even. Then, to add soldiers to finished café curtains, have your local copy center (like Kinko's Copy Store) enlarge clip art soldiers to fit within the 6" hem. Do not let soldiers go above stitch line as the rest of the picture may get cut off when being pressed on. The soldiers on our valance measure about 4 ½".

Detail of hem and soldiers.

Candy canes before dinner? When they're blue, you bet—especially when one's tongue turns such a nifty sickly shade!

Decorating for Christmas

Soldier Boy Gift Stack

This cute little soldier boy will guard those precious gifts until it is time for unwrapping. Well, not really, but at least he makes for an interesting display piece while the gifts do remain in their wrapping.

Materials

- 12" straw wreath
- 2 cardboard cakes circles (8"-diameter)
- ½-yard 36"-long red felt
- 9" x 12" royal blue felt piece
- ⅔-yard white "flapper" fringe
- 2 yards white gimp trim
- ⅓-yard black gimp
- 2 yards red-and-white cording with lip
- 5" polystyrene ball (head)
- 2" polystyrene ball (cut in half for cheeks)
- 1½" polystyrene ball (nose)
- 19" polystyrene egg
- 2-oz. bottle flesh-colored acrylic paint by Plaid
- 2-oz. bottle red acrylic paint by Plaid
- 2½ c. flour
- 2 c. water
- Newspaper
- 2 holly buttons
- 2 red ¾" buttons
- 10"-square cardboard piece
- 2 black marabou 6-foot feather boas
- 1 package 1" Comical Eyes by Bel-Tree
- ½"-diameter wooden dowel (at least 6" long)
- Several 2" nails with heads
- Double-sided sticky tape
- 3 toothpicks
- Paintbrush
- Serrated kitchen knife
- Several straight pins
- Handsaw
- Scissors or rotary cutter
- Ice pick
- Hot glue gun and glue sticks
- Patterns (page 117)

For the head:

1. Hot glue 1½" polystyrene ball to middle of larger "head" ball for nose.

2. With serrated knife, cut 2" polystyrene ball in half. Hot glue half of ball to face on either side of nose for cheeks using toothpicks to hold in place. Set aside. (Spaces will be covered by papier-mâché later.)

3. Trim 2" off of pointed end of polystyrene egg.

4. Trim top of head to flatten it. The flat areas of egg and head should be equal.

5. Hot glue and toothpick egg to head.

6. Cut wooden dowel to 6" length and insert halfway into bottom of head for the neck.

7. Secure dowel with hot glue. This is useful for holding the head while applying papier-mâché and paint.

8. Tear newspaper into small pieces.

9. Mix equal amounts of flour and water for paste. Add more flour if too runny.

10. Dip newspaper squares into flour and water paste and apply to face area only, as shown at right. Do not include hat. Smooth to retain the shape of nose and cheeks. Allow to dry.

11. Paint newspaper-covered face with two coats of flesh-colored paint. Allow to dry.

12. Add a bit of red paint to a small amount of the flesh color. Use this blush color to paint two circles for cheeks and a small circle at tip of nose. Let dry.

13. Starting in back, where polystyrene egg meets head, pin one end of marabou boa and tightly wrap around. Hold with pins along the way as needed. Repeat with second boa to finish.

Noël Note:

Your Soldier Boy can easily be turned into a wall-mounted wreath by removing the two cake circles and filling in the blank space with an arrangement of Christmas foliage, small wrapped packages, or toys.

Christopher plays it safe, giving his gift a good shake before opening.

For arms:

1. Saw bottom from straw wreath, creating two flat ends or "stubs."

2. Stitch ⅓" x 36" red felt lengthwise into sleeve. Turn right-side out and slip onto wreath "stubs".

3. Hot glue each flat wreath "stub" to center of an individual cardboard cake circle. Push 2" nails up from bottom to help hold the two stubs in place. Your soldier's "arms" should now stand on their own.

4. At top of wreath, use an ice pick to bore a hole down through the felt and into center. Do not bore all the way through to the bottom, but do make hole big enough to accommodate wooden dowel "neck."

5. Fill hole with hot glue and insert wooden dowel neck on the soldier's head. Leave about 1" of dowel exposed between arms and head.

For the collar:

1. Using the pattern on page 117, cut two collar pieces from red felt.

2. Sandwich the red-and-white cording inside the two collar pieces so that the cording's lip and the collar edges line up. Stitch using a zipper foot, being sure to leave a small opening for turning.

3. Turn collar and press flat.

4. Put collar around Soldier Boy's neck and stitch front together to close.

5. Add a bit of hot glue to base of collar to help hold in place.

6. With hot glue, add holly buttons to collar and red buttons to front of sleeve under chin.

For epaulets:

1. Cut two epaulets from cardboard using pattern on page 117.

2. Cut four matching pieces (top and bottom) from royal blue felt.

3. Hold felt in place on top and bottom of cardboard with double-sided tape.

4. Whipstitch epaulet edges.

5. Cut white fringe in half and hot glue around wide end of each epaulet so it hangs down free.

6. Use hot glue to secure red-and-white braid and white gimp to top edge of epaulets.

7. Hot glue epaulets to either "shoulder."

8. The Soldier Boy is well-laden with blue and red wrapped packages, which cover his cake circle base. He sits atop other patriotically wrapped packages.

More Christmas Decorating Ideas

Just in case you haven't got quite enough inspiration for making your home its festive best, here are a few extra projects that can really go with any decoration scheme and in any room.

Four-by-Four Wreath

Our wreath is called "Four-by-Four" because everything is done in fours. We have used traditional holiday flowers and berries, but you can change yours as you like. Let ours be a guide for your own imagination. Instead of the usual, try clustering vintage felt elves on plastic foam "snowballs" or tuck antique postcards in and around the greenery.

Wreath Decorating 101

Keep in mind that nothing truly looks worse on a wreath than a pinecone, pinecone, pinecone evenly spaced around it, followed by a poinsettia, poinsettia, poinsettia, holly leaf, holly leaf, holly... well, you get the idea. Learn to cluster your chosen items into one concentrated area of the wreath—top, bottom, or side—for the greatest impact.

Materials

- 20" natural or artificial wreath
- 4 small grape clusters
- 4 pink roses
- 4 pink rosebuds
- 4 blue hydrangeas
- 4 pinecones
- 4 red berry clusters
- 4 frosted ivy leaf picks

- 4 each small, medium, and large red Christmas balls*
- Hot glue gun and glue sticks
- Scissors
- 3" piece 18-gauge wire (optional)

*The plastic ones that look like glass are best.

1. Using a scissors, remove heads of flowers from stems.

2. Beginning at bottom of wreath, use the hot glue gun to secure the larger items such as hydrangea, rose heads, and pinecones in tight knit groups onto wreath. Refer to the project photo for guidance, if necessary.

3. Fill in with the other items, leaving the red berries and Christmas balls for last so their bright colors really stand out.

4. Hang on door or wall either by resting the inner ring of the wreath on a hook or nail, or attach a loop of wire to the back of the wreath and hang from the wire.

Decorating for Christmas

Snowman Wreath

The poem "Stopping by the Woods on a Snowy Evening" by Robert Frost comes to mind as the sun does its best to melt our frosty friend.

Mark first created this special holiday wreath several years ago. This one and others have been featured in many craft and decorating venues, including the "Carol Duval Show." Instructions for his Santa Wreath and 11 others, can be found in *Character Wreaths*, available at fine book and craft stores, Amazon.com, and Krause Publications at (800) 345-3168.

Materials

- 12" straw wreath
- 10" straw wreath
- 6" polystyrene ball
- Large doll-size top hat (to fit ball)
- 2 cans DAPtex Insulating Foam Sealant
- ¾-yard 1"-thick batting

- 1 tube Creative Beginnings Ultra Fine Green Diamond Dust Glitter
- 1 package #033 Sweet Potato Sculpey III
- 2½" nail
- 3" bird's nest
- 2 birds

- 3 stems artificial holly
- 12 glittery plastic snowflakes
- 1 roll packing tape
- Serrated kitchen knife
- Several straight pins
- Large plastic bag
- Scissors or rotary cutter
- Hot glue gun and glue sticks

For the main body:

1. Place the 10" wreath on top of the 12" wreath so it just overlaps onto the straw.

2. Mark your cutting lines on 12" wreath (where the 10" wreath overlaps) and cut away entire section.

3. Tape the raw ends to keep straw from coming out.

4. Abut the 12" wreath to the 10" wreath and securely tape both together. Set aside.

5. Use a serrated knife to trim about one-quarter off the backside of the polystyrene ball to make it flat. Use the knife to also curve the bottom of the ball to match the curve of the 10" wreath.

6. Drive the 2½" nail halfway into the top of the snowman's midsection (10" wreath) and secure with hot glue.

7. Drip more hot glue over nail and push the polystyrene ball head into place matching cut-out curve to top of wreath. If it isn't perfect, don't worry because it will be filled with "snow."

8. Cut batting into five 5" x 45" strips.

9. Pin end of one strip to back of 10" wreath and wrap snugly around. Pin off and start another strip, continuing until you have covered the wreath completely. Repeat for 12" wreath, but do not wrap head.

10. Take snowman outdoors and place it flat on large plastic bag to protect work surface.

11. Starting with head, cover snowman with DAPtex Insulating Foam Sealant (leave back side clean). The DAPtex will rise like shaving cream. It will also leave points every time you stop spraying. Fold these points into the rest of the DAPtex while still wet.

12. Immediately sprinkle glitter onto wet DAPtex so it will adhere.

13. Allow to dry 24 hours without touching.

For the nose:

1. Take about half of the Sculpey III and roll it out to the length of carrot nose you want. Ours is about 5½" long and 1" diameter at the larger end. As you roll, taper it to a point to resemble a carrot.

2. When in desired shape, lightly imprint Sculpey carrot all over with a fingernail, giving it the look of a carrot.

3. Bake according to package instructions and allow to cool.

Finishing the project:

1. When main body has dried and carrot nose has cooled, bore a hole with carrot end about ½" into polystyrene ball, remove, and fill hole with hot glue.

2. Push nose back into hole and hold in place until dry.

3. Crumple doll top hat to give it an aged look, place on head at a rakish angle, and hot glue to hold.

4. Perch a bright red cardinal on the brim of the hat with some holly and a squirt or two of the DAPtex "snow." Hot glue to hold.

5. Hot glue the bird's nest into place.

6. With hot glue, add bluebird and holly, as shown below.

Detail of nest.

7. Scatter the dozen large snowflakes about the snowman by sticking them into the DAPtex and hot gluing them into place.

Noël Note:

If needed, quilt pins buried in the DAP snow will help hold things in place. If the snowflakes don't seem to be holding well, go back and add another squirt of DAPtex where they're attached.

For the knit scarf:

Materials

- 1 pair #15 knitting needles
- 1 crochet hook
- 1 skein brown yarn
- 1 skein red yarn

1. Knitting loosely with both red and brown yarns at the same time, cast on 14 stitches.

2. Row 1, knit.

3. Row 2, purl.

4. Repeat until scarf is about 4 feet long.

5. Bind off.

6. Cut 28 6"-lengths of red yarn and the same number and size in brown yarn. Since there are 14 stitches on each end of the scarf, we will add fringe to each of these stitches.

7. Put one red and one brown length of yarn together and fold in the middle.

8. Insert crochet hook from underside of bottom stitch of scarf, hook the folded yarn, and pull back halfway through the stitch.

9. Remove hook and insert into the loop just created. Pull the four yarn ends through the loop.

10. Gently pull on the yarn, securing it to the scarf.

11. Repeat in every stitch at both ends of the scarf. Trim ends evenly.

12. Place scarf around your snowman's neck to keep him warm.

We Three Gilded Kings

We Three Gilded Kings roam over the sand dunes at Malibu, California, which doubles beautifully for the sands of the Sahara. We were lucky enough to find these three kings in a thrift store, a bit battered and a ghastly shade of blue. But with a little TLC, these— or any candlestick or figurine—may be gilded by the following process, creating a stunning holiday decoration.

Noël Note:

Just in case you wanted to know, frankincense (as well as myrrh) is an aromatic gum resin found in certain trees in Asia and Africa. It is chiefly used in religious practices and in the making of pharmaceuticals and perfumes.

Materials

- Candlesticks or figurines of choice
- 1 jar Plaid Liquid Leaf Florentine Gold
- 2-oz. bottle Nutmeg FolkArt Acrylic Paint by Plaid
- 2-oz. bottle Red FolkArt Acrylic Paint by Plaid
- FolkArt Eggshell Crackle Kit by Plaid
- ½"-wide paintbrush
- Anita's Gold Foil Leafing Kit
- 1 can High Gloss Clear Glaze by Chase Color-Spray
- 2 red taper candles
- Mineral spirits or turpentine

1. Paint candlesticks with Plaid Liquid Leaf Florentine Gold and allow to dry.

2. Apply FolkArt Eggshell Crackle according to instructions on bottle.

3. Mix two parts red paint to one part brown paint and thin with water to consistency of milk.

4. Brush paint onto candlestick and immediately wipe off, leaving reddish paint in crackle and crevices.

5. Apply gold foil leafing to most areas, following instructions on package.

6. Clean brushes with mineral spirits or turpentine.

7. Spray two thin coats of Clear Glaze over the entire candlestick, waiting 45 minutes between coats.

8. Insert candles and display.

Before and after shots above. Note the broken nose on the one plaster king. The following process easily covers up small imperfections (such as cracks), giving new life to favorite finds. Displayed on a gilded mirror (with a bit of that "Egyptian" sand, as shown in the photo on the previous page), their golden light is reflected about the room.

Detail of We Three Kings Candlestick.

Of Christmas Interest

Nowhere in the Bible is it stated that only three kings (or wise men) visited the Christ Child. These details to the birth of Jesus have been added through the years by other sources. In Matthew 2:1 it states: "...there came wise men from the east to Jerusalem..." Some religions claim that as many as 12 wise men made the journey.

The assumption that there were only three is due largely to the fact that Matthew states three gifts were brought: gold, frankincense and myrrh.

The names of the kings—Gaspar, Melchior, and Balthasar—are also not from the Bible. The very first appearance of these names is not until 500 years after the birth of Christ. Although legend has it that Gaspar, bearer of the frankincense, was the king of Tarsus, Melchior, who brought gold, was king of Arabia, and Balthasar, the king of Ethiopia, arrived bearing myrrh.

Nowhere does the Bible depict the wise men as kings. Many scientists feel they were probably learned astrologers. The Bible also says nothing about the wise men arriving the night of Christ's birth, but rather that they met him as a "young child" (Matthew 2:11). After all, if one was following a star more than 2,000 years ago, travel is going to take some time!

Decorating for Christmas

Clay Pot Angels

Hang these little ethereal beings with their halos askew all over the place, but remember to watch out for those little lighted candles.

Materials

- 1¼" wooden doll head
- ½" wooden doll head
- 1¾" high clay pot
- 9" to 12" floral wire
- 2 1¾" wooden light bulbs (flat on one side)
- 1¼" wooden ring
- 4"-wide set wooden angel wings
- 2-oz. bottle Delta Ceramcoat red acrylic paint
- Birthday candle
- Black Sharpie pen
- Drill and ⅛" drill bit
- Paintbrush
- Hot glue gun and glue sticks
- Earthquake putty or hot wax (optional)

1. With ⅛" drill bit, drill wooden doll head all the way through top, starting at existing hole in flat of larger doll head.

2. For feet together, sandwich 1" of wire between the two wooden light bulbs and hot glue flat sides together, as shown at right.

3. Tie large knot in wire 1" above wooden feet.

4. Thread wire through clay pot and angel head, securing flattened side of wooden head to clay pot.

5. On top of head, form 1" loop of wire and twist, shown lower right.

6. Use Sharpie to draw desired face on head.

7. Water down red acrylic and paint on for cheeks.

8. Glue wooden ring (halo) at jaunty angle atop head.

9. Hot glue wings to back of clay pot so the bottoms of wings rest on clay pot ridge.

10. Hot glue ½" wooden doll head, flat side up, to front of clay pot "dress." Make sure it rests on clay pot ridge.

11. Secure tiny birthday candle inside small wooden ball with hot glue, hot wax, or earthquake putty.

For feet-apart variation:

1. Follow step 1 as before.
2. For feet apart, cut 12" of wire.
3. Hot glue ends of wire to flat backs of each light bulb, as shown.
4. Pinch wire together to form knots 1" above wooden feet.
5. Thread wire up through pot and wooden angel head.
6. Form 1" loop and twist.
7. Continue with steps 6 through 11 as before.

Caution: *Lit candles should be watched at all times. Never hang lit candles on Christmas trees. Birthday candles only burn from seven to 10 minutes and Clay Pot Angel should not be hung below or near anything flammable.*

Noël Note:

In 1836, Alabama was the first state to pass a law making Christmas a legal holiday.

While you're hauling out the holly, be sure to bring out all your favorite Christmas books, including your newest favorite—this one! With covers, stories, and titles depicting the holiday season, they make fine decorations that are also rather useful for putting the little ones to sleep on Christmas Eve so you can get back downstairs and start putting that bicycle together!

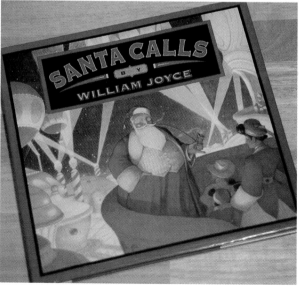

Johnny Snowman

Materials

- Large Quaker Oatmeal cardboard container
- 1 sheet (12" x 18") white Foamies by Darice
- 2 sheets (9" x 12") black Foamies by Darice
- Large bag Neon Pom-Poms by Darice (assorted colors)
- 2 oval 20mm wiggle eyes by Darice
- 9" x 12" kelly green felt piece
- ¼-yard 36"-wide red felt
- Holly leaf pattern (page 116)
- Small plate
- Scissors
- Hot glue gun and glue sticks

What better way to hide all those "toity" necessities than with a jaunty Johnny Snowman? Your bathroom will look neat and orderly and that extra roll of toilet paper or your room spray will be quick at hand.

1. Empty the Quaker Oats container and discard lid.

2. Wrap white Foamies sheet around container, trim, and hot glue in place.

3. For earmuffs, hot glue a large neon green pom-pom over each "ear," as shown at right.

4. To form "carrot" nose, start with the largest neon orange pom-pom. Hot glue two large ones together, then two medium, and finally two small pom-poms, all in a row. Hot glue to center of face.

5. Hot glue the two wiggle eyes onto either side of the carrot nose.

6. For hat brim, using small plate as a pattern, cut an 8" circle from one black Foamies sheet.

7. Hot glue brim circle to top of snowman.

8. Roll the second black Foamies sheet into a tube that will accommodate a spray can of air freshener, trim, and hot glue together to hold.

9. Cut a 1" square out of top backside of tube for easier access to spray can. Hot glue tube on top of hat brim.

10. For scarf, trim red felt down to 7" width and fringe ends.

11. Wrap scarf piece around bottom of container, holding it in place with hot glue. Knot ends to one side and allow excess scarf to hang.

12. Using the green felt, cut four holly leaves using the pattern on page 116.

13. Pinch together holly leaves at bottom with a dab of hot glue.

14. Hot glue two leaves to scarf knot and two more leaves to opposite side of hat.

15. Hot glue three neon pink pom-pom "berries" to each holly leaf cluster.

Noël Note:

Don't pack away those leftover ornament hangers when the holidays are over. They can be pretty useful in craft and decorating projects all year long.

Hiding It All Away

Decorating for Christmas

All patterns are 100% unless noted otherwise.

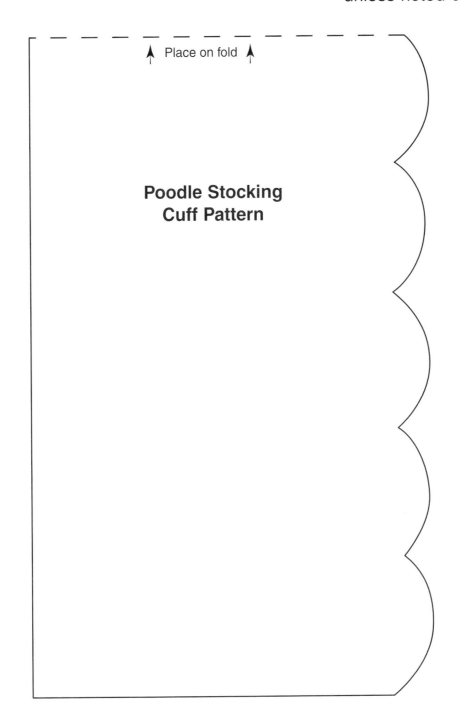

Place on fold

**Poodle Stocking
Cuff Pattern**

Lasertran Santa Stocking and Poodle Stocking Pattern

Enlarge 150%.
Cut 2.

Trace pattern and join together here.

Decorating for Christmas

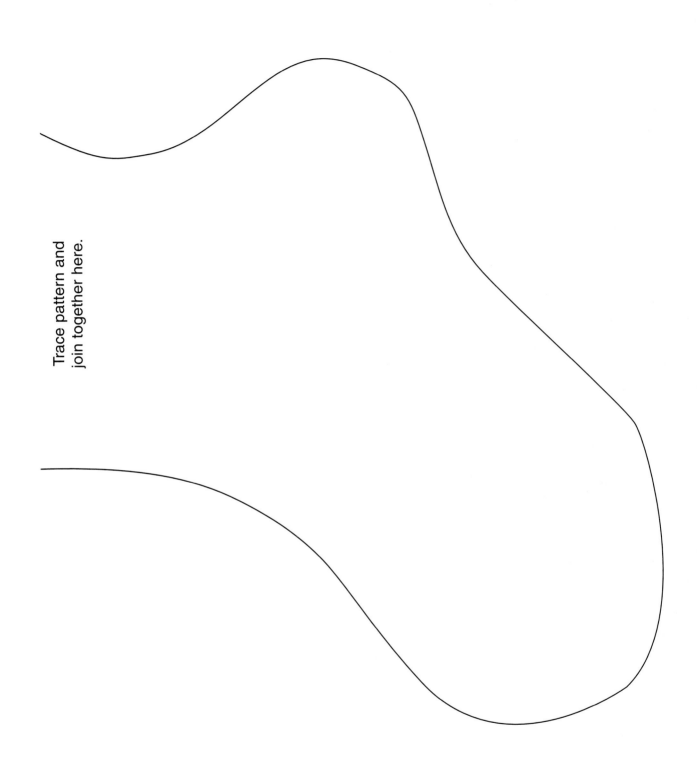

Trace pattern and join together here.

Poodle Tree Skirt Patterns

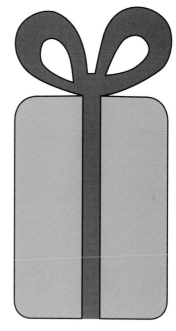

Medium Package

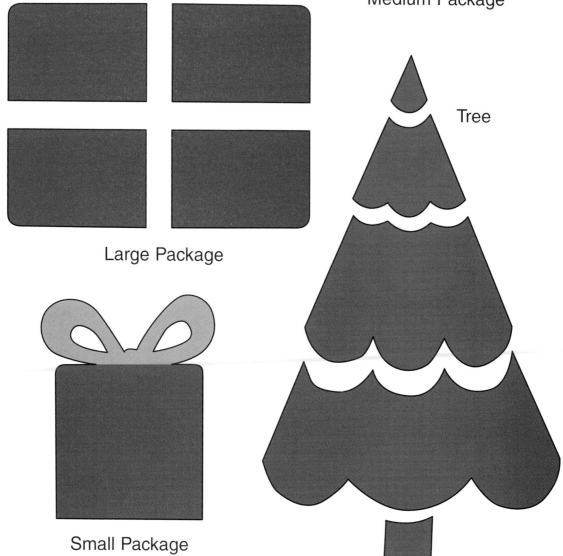

Large Package

Tree

Small Package

Decorating for Christmas

Poodle Tree Skirt Patterns

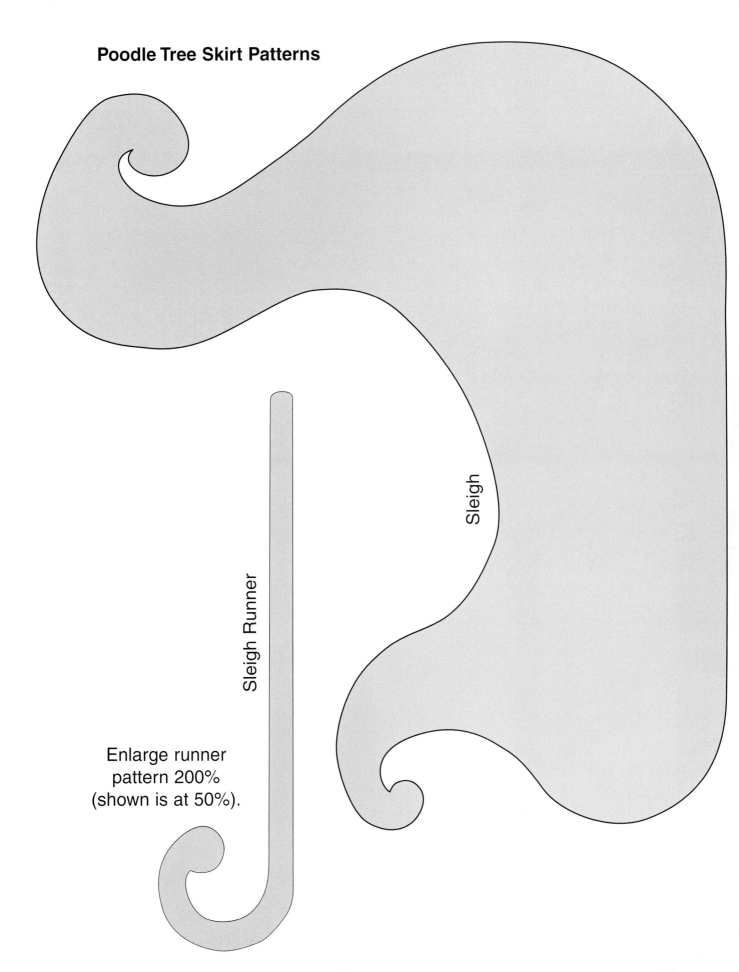

Sleigh

Sleigh Runner

Enlarge runner
pattern 200%
(shown is at 50%).

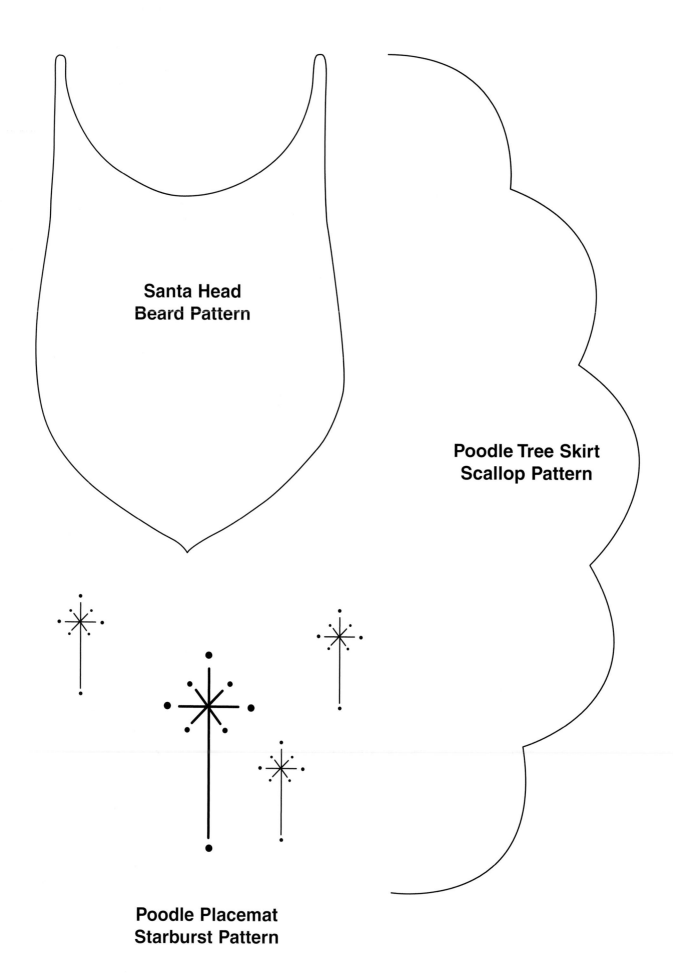

**Santa Head
Beard Pattern**

**Poodle Tree Skirt
Scallop Pattern**

**Poodle Placemat
Starburst Pattern**

Decorating for Christmas

Poodle Pad Patterns

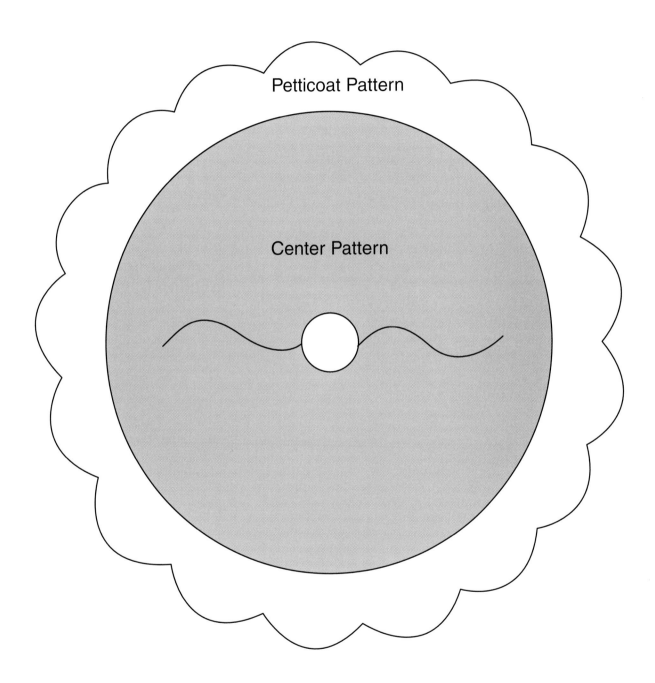

Petticoat Pattern

Center Pattern

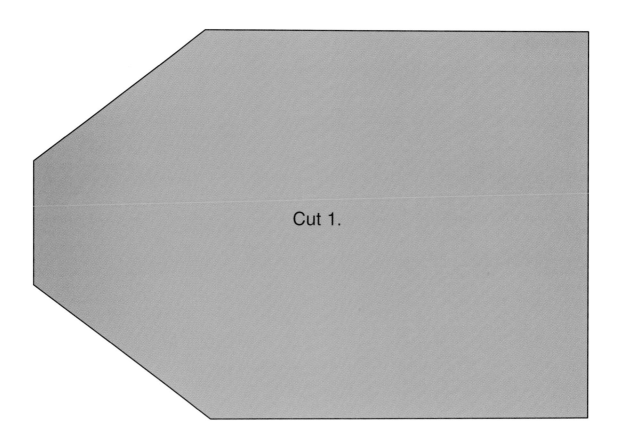

Cut 1.

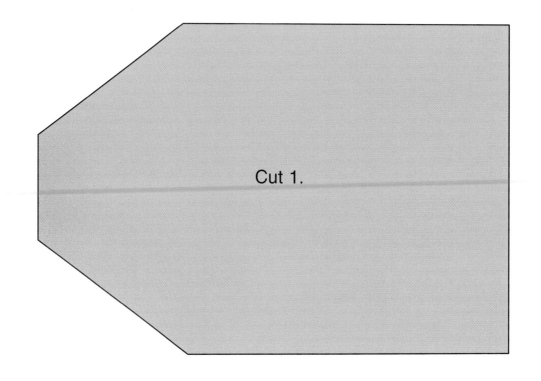

Cut 1.

Poodle Pocket Apron
Pattern (Hers)

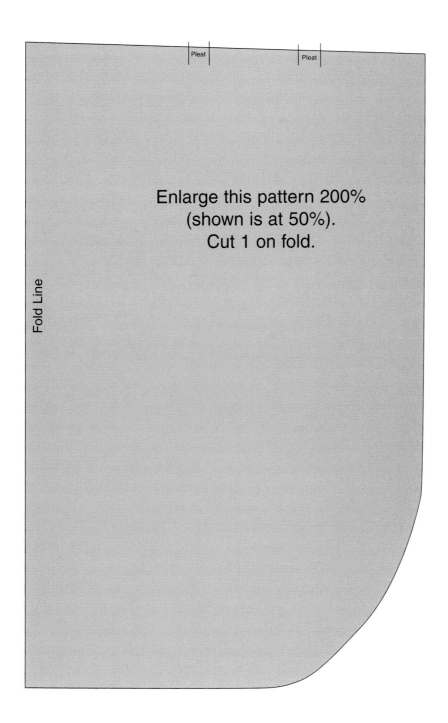

Pleat   Pleat

Enlarge this pattern 200%
(shown is at 50%).
Cut 1 on fold.

Fold Line

Poodle Pocket Apron
Pocket Pattern

Cut 1.

Decorating for Christmas

Dutch Mitten Pattern

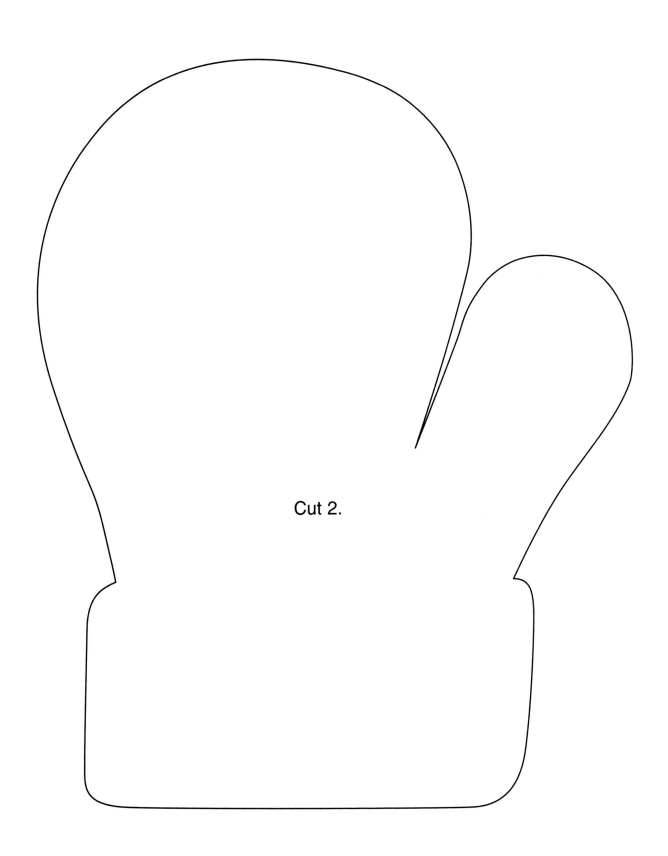

Cut 2.

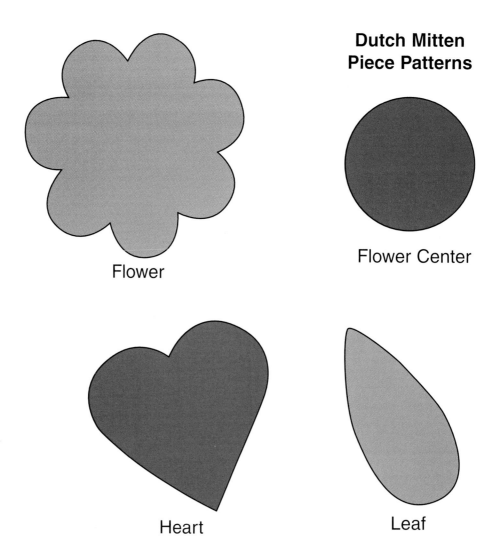

**Dutch Mitten
Piece Patterns**

Flower

Flower Center

Heart

Leaf

**Johnny Snowman
Leaf Pattern**

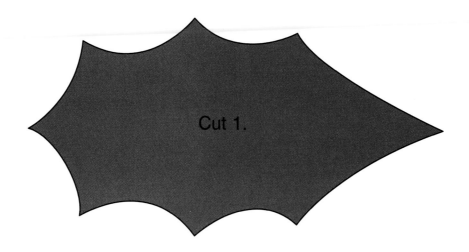

Cut 1.

Soldier Boy Gift Stack Patterns

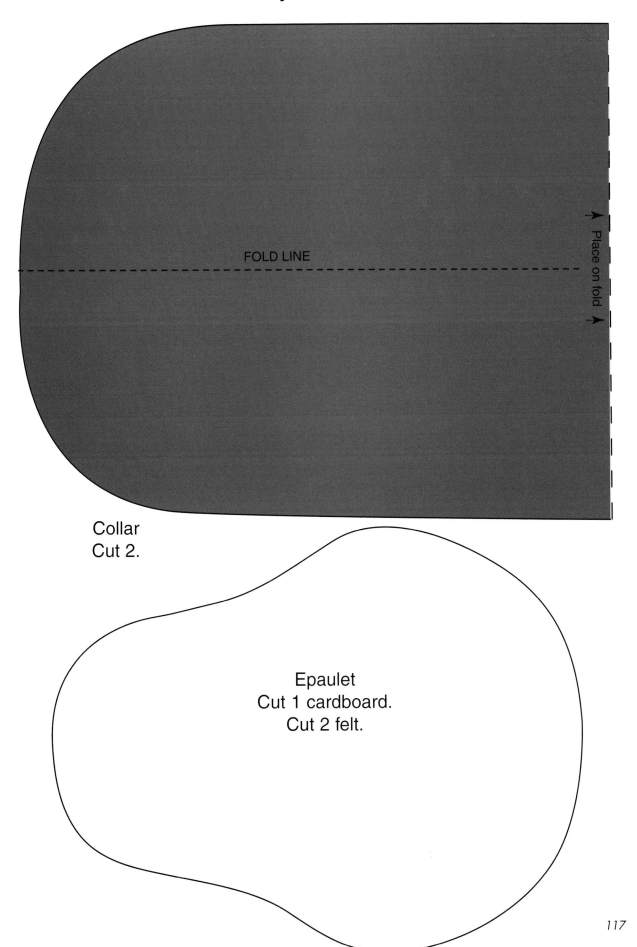

FOLD LINE

Place on fold

Collar
Cut 2.

Epaulet
Cut 1 cardboard.
Cut 2 felt.

Vintage Santa Clip Art

Note: All Santa clip art is
reproduced with permission from
Dover Publications.

Decorating for Christmas

Decorating for Christmas

Resources

Following is a list of our suppliers—including the names of the business sites where we conducted several of our photo shoots. When possible we have given the company name, address, contact number and Web site. Please keep in mind that most of the products used in this book are readily available at most craft and hobby stores, such as Michael's, JoAnn's, Home Depot, and even the local grocery store.

We hope that you, dear reader, will search out these very special products to use in your holiday decorating and everyday crafting as we found they are quite simply the very best!

Aileene's
5673 Shields Avenue
Fresno, CA 93727
Phone: (900) 388-1000
Web site:
        www.duncancrafts.com
Glues and hot glue guns.
Available at your local
craft stores.

Bob's Candies
P.O. Box 3170
Albany, GA 31706
Phone: (800) 569-4033
Web site:
        www.bobscandies.com

Chase Products
P. O. Box 70
Maywood, IL 60153
e-mail: TeresaEsposito@
        chaseproducts.com
Glitter spray and spray snow.
"Putting the best at your
fingertips."

Creative Beginnings
Diamond Dust Glitter.
Phone: (800) 367-1739

DAPtex Insulating Foam Sealant
2400 Boston Street
#200
Baltimore, MD 21224
Phone: (888) dap-tips
Web site: www.dap.com

Graphic Products Corporation
455 Maple Avenue
Carpentersville, IL 60110
Phone: (847) 836-9600
Fax: (847) 836-9666
e-mail: info@gpcpapers.com
Decorative Accents Paper Leaves.

Dover Publications, Inc.
Dept. 23
31 E. 2nd Street
Mineola, NY 11501
Clip art books.

Eagle Brand
735 Taylor Road
Columbus, OH 43230
Web site: www.eaglebrand.com
Mouth-watering recipes;
cookbook available.

Ed DeBevic's Restaurant
134 N. La Cienega
Beverly Hills, CA 90211
Phone: (310) 659-1952

Houseworks, Ltd.
2388 Pleasantdale Road
Atlanta, GA 30340
Phone: (770) 448-6596
Scale model mesh mounted
brick sheets.

Judy's Designs
109 W. 2nd Street
Loveland, CO 80537
Phone: (970) 622-9717
Fax: (970) 622-9863
Charming wooden birdhouses,
carved trees, and miniature
accessories.

Kinko's Copy Stores
To locate store nearest you,
please call: (800) 254-6567

Christmas by Krebs
3911 S. Main Street
Roswell, NM 88203
Phone: (505) 624-2882
Lovely Christmas ornaments
available nationally in stores
throughout the Christmas season.
We even use orange, purple,
and green for Halloween.

Lazertran Papers
650 8th Street
New Hyde Park, NY 11040
Fax: (516) 488-7898
e-mail: mic.@lazertran.com

La Vogue Blumenthal Lansing Co.
La Vogue Appliqué
1929 Main Street
Lansing, IA 52161
Phone: (201) 935-6220
e-mail: appliq@laueswww.buttonsplus.com
Pink iron-on poodles.

Libbey, Inc.
300 Madison Avenue
Toledo, OH 43604
Phone: (419) 325-2100

K'Nex Industries, Inc.
2990 Bergey Road
Hatfield, PA 19440-0700
Phone: (800) 543-5639
Fax: (215) 996-4222
Web site: www.knex.com
Lincoln Logs Commemorative
Collectors Set (in original-
looking tin).

Log Cabin Syrup
Everyone's favorite since
childhood. Available nationally
at supermarkets, mom-and-pop
stores, and most restaurants over
hotcakes.

Modern Options
(a division of Triangle Coatings)
2831 Merced Street
San Leandro, CA 94577
Phone: (510) 895-8000
e-mail: info@modernoptions.com
Web site:
          www.modernoptions.com
Patina Antiquing Kit and
Instant Rust Kit.

Mummert Sign Company
511 W. King Street
P.O. Box 69
East Berlin, PA 17316
Phone: (717) 259-8055
Fax: (717) 259-5455
Vintage rusty signs.

Ohio Wholesale, Inc.
Phone: (877) 745-5050
Web site:
          www.ohiowholesale.com
Oodles of charming Americana,
rusty tin signs, angels, pictures,
and more.

Plaid Enterprises
3225 Westech Drive
Norcross, GA 30092
Phone: (800) 842-4197
Web site: www.plaidonline.com
Great paints and crackle coats.

Plasti-kote Division
Phone: (800) 328-8044
Fleckstone, Clear Kote Spray,
and other great finishes.

SnoWonder
90 Lions Field Drive
Santa Cruz, CA 95065
Phone: (866) 363-3807
Fax: (831) 724-0165
Web site: www.sno-wonder.com
"Real" artificial snow – lasts
indefinitely.

*Kasey and Christmas go way back. In
the mid-1950s, she made a three-reel
View Master set depicting the Nativity.
No, that is not Mark in the manger!*

Stage Coach Inn and
Newbury House Museum
51 S. Ventu Park Road
Newberry Park, CA 91320
Phone: (805) 498-9441

Tender Heart Treasures
10917 Harry Watanabe Parkway
Omaha, NE 68128
Phone: (800) 443-1367
Fax: (900) 593-1316
Web site: www.tenderheart.com
e-mail: tht@tenderheart.com
Wonderful collection of
"treasures," including the
vintage mail holder and cute
bear cub, both used in our
Country Cabin Christmas.

Ghosts of Christmases Past

Invite the ghosts of Christmases past to your next holiday festivities. And, what better decoration to use than heirloom children photos? Those taken at Christmas or with winter themes are best, but we used a rather bewitching assortment of characters. Can you name the people in these pictures?

Answers: *From left: "Dr. Bombay" himself, Bernard Fox; Kasey at 3 years old (Hard to believe they even had film then!); Dick Sargent ("Darrin #2"); and Sandra Gould ("Gladys Kravitz") at sweet 16!*